RAISED IN THE
SHADOW OF THE BOMB
CHILDREN OF THE MANHATTAN PROJECT

To the South Brunswick Public Library

D. Leah Steinberg
8/24/20

D. LEAH STEINBERG

ya
nf

Printed in the United States of America

Published by:
Ingram Spark
Deborah Leah Steinberg
Email: raisedintheshadowofthebomb@gmail.com
Web site: http://www.raisedintheshadowofthebomb.com

First Edition: November 2016

ISBN 978-0-9983006-0-3

Cover and book design by Bob Minkin / http://www.minkindesign.com

Cover photographs:
Hiroshima blast, August 6, 1945.

Aerial view of ground zero at the Trinity site test, the world's first nuclear test of "the gadget", Alamogordo, New Mexico July 16, 1945. Courtesy of Los Alamos Historical Society Archives.

The author age five.

The author's father, Ellis P. Steinberg, age 23, at the University of Chicago during the Manhattan Project.

"Your descendants shall gather your fruits."

—Virgil

Contents

Part IV - My (Extended) Nuclear Family

Acknowledgments

Thank you to my brother, David Steinberg, and sister, Sheri Steinberg, and my cousins Abigail Abraham, Jesse Abraham, and Daniel Abraham, for sharing your views with me.

Thank you to all who took the time to speak with me and allowed me to interview them.

Thank you to all those who encouraged me, beyond all hope, that I could complete this.

I acknowledge all present and future residents of this planet in the hope that we will survive as a species.

Dedication

~~~

To my father, Ellis P. Steinberg; my mother, Esther (Terry) Abraham Steinberg; and my uncle Bernard Abraham.

With special gratitude to Dana Mitchell.

To all the scientists, engineers, technical support people, and staff of the Manhattan Project.

To the Japanese people who died or suffered lifelong diseases as a result of the bombings of Hiroshima and Nagasaki.

To all the unknown victims of plutonium and radiation experiments.

Preface

Chapter Zero

"Poets say science takes away from the beauty of the
stars—mere globs of gas atoms. I, too, can see the stars on
a desert night, and feel them. But do I see less or more?"
—*Richard P. Feynman*

My whole life I have walked with one foot in and one foot
out of doomsday. From early childhood I felt disconnected
from my family and the world, and my personal, psychological, familial, political, and spiritual pilgrimage paralleled the
journey of the world into the nuclear age.

This story began before I was born when my father, Ellis
P. Steinberg, worked on the Manhattan Project—the secret
undertaking that developed the first atomic bombs, which
were dropped over Hiroshima and Nagasaki. Growing up
after World War II, I shared an atomic bond with my siblings,
cousins, parents, aunt, and uncle. Only I, however, felt an ele-
mental identification with both the unprecedented brilliance
of this scientific achievement and the destructive power it
unleashed. I took on guilt that was not mine.

The image of an atom being split resonated with me, and
I felt compelled to put myself back together and understand
and make peace with my personal and familial association
with the oxymoronic creation of the bomb.

Recently I was glancing through old photos and found

a picture of myself in my crib. Above my head the wall was bare except for a pennant from Deep River. I had to look closely to see that it said "Chalk River, Ontario." I discovered this was the site of the first Canadian nuclear power plant and a nuclear accident had taken place there in 1952, the year of my birth.

Many decades later, the idea for my book was sparked by a cartoon drawn by my cousin after an anti-nuclear march. I took the cartoon home with me on a yellow school bus, back through the cornfields of my youth to the lakes surrounding Madison, Wisconsin. My vision of the book became at once more diffuse and more detailed and complex.

I thought I wanted validation and hoped to attribute my problems to my father and the bomb. I had explained away my pain and confusion by the reality of being too close to the core of the most destructive weapon ever created. But life is not that simple, nor, I suppose, should it be.

Another aspect of myself that led me to write this book was my belief that there may be just beneath our consciousness a story—the true legacy of the context of our everyday lives and political reality begun during the Manhattan Project that merged pure science and the military in a Faustian bond that has kept us in its grip ever since.

Secret work cast an invisible shadow over everyday life—school, concerts, picnics, baseball, and shopping—in the landscape of 1950s and '60s America. We, the "children," were closer to the legacy of the secret and the possibility of nuclear annihilation than others.

I realized it was not only my extended nuclear family that experienced and was affected by growing up at this time in history, but that there was a whole generation of other children raised in the shadow of the bomb who had stories to tell.

As I interviewed them, I realized that, along with the pride we had in our parents' accomplishments, the common work they engaged in affected us all—in the values we adopted, the careers we chose, and the ways we became citizens of the world. Many of us felt acutely the conflict between scientific research and the political and military applications of its discoveries that still exists in the threat of nuclear war, a threat that is as real as it was seventy years ago.

This book is not a scientific study with a control group. I cannot extrapolate global results from having a parent who worked on the A-bomb. I can only share my stories and those of my cohorts, many now friends, who said yes when I asked to talk with them. I'd known five almost since birth and met the others in various ways: through the Manhattan Project website, at the 2005 60th anniversary reunion in Oak Ridge, Tennessee, and by chance.

This book is about pride, doubt, fear, regret, and a search for understanding and forgiveness. It is about secrets kept, atoms shattered, the conflagration of thermonuclear weapons, and a cold peace. It is about the legacy we grew up with and what we leave to our children.

The landscape of nuclear disaster goes deeper than the release of radiation. It permeates our consciousness and enters our hearts, becoming part of our way of thinking, speaking, and living. I feel the threat and uncertainty that continues to hover over the future. I know I am not alone.

"Come wash the nighttime clean,
Come grow the scorched ground green."

Words by John Barlow [1]

Part I

Elements of Self

Chapter 1

In the Shadows

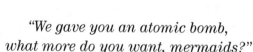

"We gave you an atomic bomb,
what more do you want, mermaids?"
—Isidor Isaac Rabi

When I was five years old I carried my small blue book bag to kindergarten in Copenhagen, learning to speak Danish but knowing nothing of atoms or fission. What I remember most is cold winds blowing from the North Sea and a bronze statue called The Little Mermaid (Den lille Havfrue) that came from the mind of Hans Christian Andersen. I gazed out to sea with her while my father spent a year working and studying at the Niels Bohr Institute.

My father helped create the first atomic bomb. Using mathematical and scientific principles to penetrate the unseen heart of matter, brilliant scientists trusted they could split apart the smallest particle then known in the universe and create something new. The innate human passion for knowledge, intellectual exchange, and understanding the mysteries of the universe was especially strong at that time, due to new and exciting advances in chemistry and physics. That knowledge came to be utilized for military and political purposes and subsequently was unleashed on the world. The conflict between pure science and the creation of increasingly destructive weapons arose from the work of Enrico Fermi, Leo Szilard, and Robert Oppenheimer, and the part my father played in that research affected him—and me—greatly.

Although I was born after World War II and the horrors of Hiroshima and Nagasaki, I deeply felt those conflicting forces of love of knowledge and destruction. If it is true that we can feel the energy around us in the womb, then my cousin's cartoon of a fetus inside an atomic bomb (See Chapter 2.) bears some truth.

In the southern suburb of Chicago where I grew up in a ranch-style house in the fifties and sixties, there was a twenty-five-mile buffer between our white middle class community and Argonne National Laboratory, where my father worked. Throughout my life, I have had both immense pride in what was accomplished in a short time with mere slide rules, intellect, and imagination and immense sadness at the suffering that resulted from the use of the A-bomb. These forces pulled me in all directions at once, though I longed to reach for the sky and all that life had to offer.

I remember wanting to be the first woman astronaut or symphony conductor, a great artist or poet, or a brilliant scholar, but was immobilized by my desires and the world I saw around me. Vietnam and the backlash against science and technology were the backdrop of my adolescence, and depression and futility colored my entire world view. I wanted to abandon it all, but still yearned for the accolades of knowledge and accomplishment. When friends became involved in the anti-nuclear movement, I became silent—partly due to a secret loyalty to my father's work in nuclear physics. Poetry, music, and dreams of a peaceful world kept me alive, but in the words of a song, there was "such a long, long time to be gone and a short time to be there."[2]

As a child, I felt a pull inside me—down into the knowledge of emptiness, the essence of ground zero, where nothing lives and nothing grows. But I did grow in knowledge and understanding. I progressed through the normal stages of elementary school, junior high, and high school. I followed my own path through the years of the civil rights movement, living in a Lutheran church on Chicago's South Side one summer after my junior year (approved by my Jewish father after a talk with the minister, George), where I was introduced to 1968 Chicago politics, volunteer work, and the Black Panthers. I attended Jesse Jackson's Operation Breadbasket Saturday morning meetings. Our small group was an island of teenage whites in a sea of black.

I campaigned for Eugene McCarthy for president in 1968 and marched against the Vietnam War. On Moratorium Day-October 15, 1969, a day of massive demonstrations across the United States to end the war—a long march down Chicago's Michigan Avenue ended at Civic Center Plaza, where the rally was supposed to occur. The Picasso cubist sculpture with two irises in its single eye stood watch over the developing police riot. As it began to rain, I escaped, running past heads being cracked and people lying on the ground bleeding. Propelled by the terror streaming though my just turned sixteen-year-old mind and body, I could not stop.

When I returned home and told my father, his response was, "What did you expect?" Maybe, on a subconscious level, I *did* seek out experiences that I thought would help me bridge the schism in a country at war with itself politically and racially and in my own dissociated self.

The path to achieve real peace for the human race, the

future of our survival, is still elusive. In my view, the energy of the split atom still holds my own and all of our shadow selves.

Chapter 2

A March and a Cartoon

～

*"I closed the door on my past, but it
crept back in the window."*
—*Itamar Yaoz-Kest* [3]

On the hot and muggy Saturday of June 12, 1982, I arrived in
New York City to meet my cousin Daniel, whose father—my
mother's brother—had worked with mine on the Manhattan
Project. I had traveled from Madison, Wisconsin, in a caravan of yellow school buses to join a gathering of sixties radi-
cals, anti-nuclear activists, environmentalists, politicians, and
hundreds of thousands of concerned citizens for an anti-nuclear march. The thirty-six-hour, thousand-mile drive across
interstates and turnpikes through the Midwest and East was
filled with political conversation, folk singing, laughing and
sign making. As we headed down the New Jersey turnpike,
I hummed Simon and Garfunkel's lyrics about searching for
America. When we arrived in Manhattan, thousands of buses
with license plates from across the country—from Wisconsin
to Texas and California to Florida—packed huge parking lots.

I met Daniel at our pre-arranged location, and we
marched together with upwards of one million people for miles
through the borough of Manhattan, down famous streets, and
past the ever-present hot dog and hot-pretzel stands to the
rally in Central Park. The day billowed with excitement and

reminded me of the protest days in Chicago when I was just a teen. The hopeful spirit of changing the world electrified the air.

The tall buildings and cement landscape made me claustrophobic. I asked Daniel, "How can you live here?" I knew his answer, though, before he spoke a word. I'd heard it before. "I love it!" he exclaimed, with a creative soul's enthusiasm for all that the city offered.

After the march and rally, Daniel and I continued our journey through his adopted city to his walk-up brownstone on the Lower East Side. Climbing the narrow, winding, seemingly never ending stairwell we arrived at the fifth floor. Immediately to the right in his tiny apartment was a kitchen barely large enough to turn around in. Ahead was his living room, and when I sat on the dark blue, secondhand, two-seated couch, it seemed like I might sink all the way down the five floors into the loud, intense, busy conversations of the New Yorkers who filled the streets.

In Daniel's bedroom, under a window that looked out over the city, stood a drawing table slanted at a 35-degree angle. In this small corner of New York, he created his art. His political cartoons would make their way into *The New Yorker*, *Rolling Stone*, and dozens of other publications.

On the floor was a small, worn rug covering an even older, dark brown wooden floor where his feet rested, one in the world of art, the other in his currently abandoned world of the law.

Without thought or discussion, Daniel picked up his sketchpad and pens, drew a picture of a fetus inside an atom bomb, and wrote "Children of the Manhattan Project" beneath it. He handed his picture to me and said, "We could have had our own contingent at the march." He ripped it out of the drawing pad with finality and a sweep of his hand that said, "This is done; time to move on." And he did, because, many years later, he would say that he did not remember drawing it.

I, however, did not move on. Daniel's illustration stirred in me a familiar dread of non-vocalized disconnectedness. It now stared at me through a cartoon out of my cousin's pen, an umbilical cord made of split atoms.

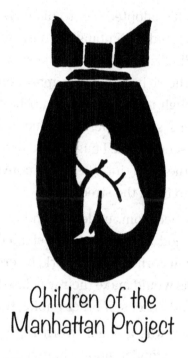

Children of the Manhattan Project

Illustration by Daniel Abraham

That five-minute cartoon expressed everything I had felt since childhood. I seemed as if I *had* grown up within the womb of the atomic bomb. I walked like a ghost in a world no one could see. I went to school, played hopscotch, skated on bumpy ponds in the winter, and graduated high school and college. But I was never really there. And it didn't really matter where I was, because there would be no place on the planet where anyone could understand this ghostly shell I inhabited. I walked in a world of shadows, carrying the burden of atomic annihilation on my shoulders. I pushed myself through the days of suburban monotony with sixties TV and the Vietnam War as a backdrop. Whenever I spoke about these thoughts to others—either children or adults—they just looked at me with questioning eyes, and I learned to not speak of such things. Family secrets should stay family secrets, I concluded, even though this secret was known to the whole world.

I surmised that these once-unspoken secrets hatched in towns that did not officially exist during World War II fester beneath all of our everyday activities, not only in me, but in our collective unconscious. An unspoken futility was cast over the planet by the birthing of the atomic bomb. For decades I would ask the same question from multiple viewpoints: could any psychologist, scientist, or musician from a dark star ever decipher this web for me? Is it possible to find my way, our way, into fusion and wholeness?

Chapter 3

One Last Item

~

*"We have what we seek. It is there all the time, and if we
give it time it will make itself known to us."*
—*Thomas Merton*

I was on my way to my childhood home in south suburban
Chicago from Madison, Wisconsin, where I had lived for a
good part of the previous twenty-five years. I drove my red,
rusted 1987 Toyota Corolla down familiar Interstates 90 and
294 toll roads through Wisconsin and Illinois, their monotony
broken seasonally by ice and snow; red, yellow, golden, or
brown leaves; and sometimes tornados. Every twenty miles I
would stop to throw coins into the same hungry, open, steel-
mouthed coin machines I had fed for decades.

After the familiar three-hour drive, I pulled onto
Westwood Street in Park Forest—home again for nearly the
last time—and walked up the driveway that had been wid-
ened twenty years before for a second car, a luxury acquired
by my mother some time in my high school days.

From the driveway I could see our one-story, three-bed-
room ranch home with its white painted panels and dark green
trim. It typified the houses described in Malvina Reynolds's
song "Little Boxes," a "ticky-tacky" frame structure that
looked just like every other one on this street and in towns

across America. I did not, however, believe that my upbringing paralleled that of much of the rest of this suburban town.

I walked past the neatly trimmed, flattop evergreens on the fifteen-foot-long walkway, perfect for the gleeful viewing of thunderstorms as a child. On that cool fall day, leaves of gold, red, and brown swirled around the lawn, falling gracefully from the oaks and maples. In the doorway, mounted outside the screen door, the mezuzah was affixed on its traditional slant, containing the rolled up Hebrew acronym for "Guardian of the doors of Israel" on one side and the Shema— the prayer central to the Jewish religion—on the other. In the hallway, I brushed past the teak dresser, brought home from our year in Denmark when my father, at the young age of thirty-seven, earned a Guggenheim Fellowship to work with physicist Niels Bohr at the Institute for Theoretical Physics in Copenhagen.

For many years the whole house was filled with furniture from our time there. This teak dresser held tablecloths, wrapping paper, a silver tray used for special occasions, and many other items not in regular use. All of these were now packed neatly in boxes scattered around the increasingly empty house.

I continued down the hallway with its two bedrooms to the right, bathroom to the left, and my parents' bedroom straight ahead. This had been my home from the ages of seven to eighteen, and my parents' home for forty-three years. My mother was finally moving to a retirement community in Walnut Creek, California, on the continuous urging of her children. She had stayed in this house for fourteen years after my father died of pancreatic cancer, caused by decades of smoking and radioactive exposure. The cancer had been determined by the Department of Labor to be related to his work on the Manhattan Project and his decades of doing research in nuclear physics and chemistry.

I stood in front of my father's closet checking to see if anything had been forgotten: a book, a photo, a sweater. On the top shelf where he had stored boxes of slides and photos through the years, was an abandoned package that looked like a couple of 8x10 photos wrapped in brown paper—probably, I thought, black-and-white pictures of the grandparents I never knew, or maybe of my father or uncles as children. These two photos had probably been in the closet since I was a child—barely one foot from the bed where I slept on the other side of the wall. As I took them out, I wondered why they were still seemingly unwrapped, the tape perfectly straight and equidistant from the precise creases—exactly how my father would have wrapped something. Had he put them away decades before and forgotten they were there? Did he want to make them look like they had never been opened? I could not understand why he would not have shown us pictures of our family.

Slowly, carefully, I unfolded the blank brown paper with no writing to identify its contents. I thought this was strange, because my father had always told me to label my photos—what they were and when they were taken—though I rarely did this.

I slowly turned them toward me. There in my hands were two color photographs that he must have thought needed no reminder of their content or where they had been taken. The first was an eerily unreal orange mushroom cloud filled with pixels of atoms—staring at me through time like a painting, beautiful in its perfection, despite its destructive power. The other photo was a view from the air of blue skies, blue sea, an island, and boats in the harbor: Bikini Atoll captured in its last moments, its partial demise rising high in the sky. It was a test, only a test that worked. Called Operation Crossroads, it took place on July 1, 1946—the first of twenty-three tests of nuclear devices over the atoll between 1946 and 1958.

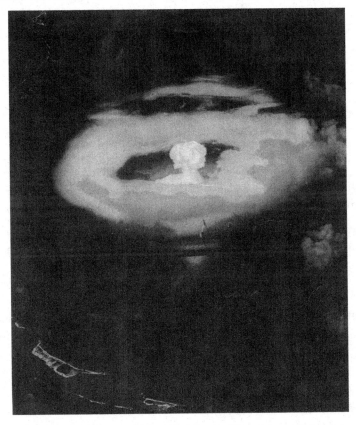

Hidden in anonymous wrapping paper, these images were separated from my childhood dreams and nightmares only by a thin wall. I put down and picked up the photos several times, then finally put them in a box and took them home.

Chapter 4

My Dream
November, 14, 2011

≋

*"Don't be afraid of the space between your
dreams and reality."*
—*Belva Davis*

I am on a large prairie, a mixture of green and brown grasses reminiscent of the flat Midwestern expanse where I grew up, when my father appears. I think there must be gophers hiding beneath the ground and am afraid my foot will get caught in one of their holes. There is a lake nearby and a dense forest of evergreens and maples in the distance. Someone herds a group of us together and shouts, "Hurry, hurry, we are leaving soon." I look at my father and he says, "I know you think I died twenty years ago. Hurry up, we are going now."

The blue horizon becomes a screen on which memories of my father appear—telling me what to do, jumping up and down like a monkey, and making funny noises that made me laugh. I remember him sitting at his desk engrossed in his work—thoughtful, tired, serious, and distant. Now he says, "You must help us with the labs above the horizon, just beyond the stratosphere. On the edge of Earth's orbit there are labs." He speaks with purpose and finality.

I look around, and there on the edge of the lake are

about seventy expressionless adults around my age, waiting for the transport. Although their faces are blank, I can still see the questions and fear hidden from view. Nearby are two dozen scientists busily talking and making plans, excited about the mission they are to embark on. They shake hands, renewing old friendships and collaborations from the early days. The excitement they exude reverses time. They stand together, representing fifty years of scientific collaboration, reunited one last time.

Then we are in the transport. Not much room for equipment, I think to myself. Up in the sky, the clouds fade away, and hundreds of laboratories slip past us. They seem grounded in nothing but gravity's pull between the earth and moon. We stop from time to time at one lab or another to organize trays of test tubes and files. I have no idea what I am doing, but even without instructions, it seems we are not making mistakes. I look around at the others, but no one says a word. My father is busily working, totally content, almost dancing around his test tubes, and not noticing my questioning eyes.

I smell the chemicals, some sweet, some sulfuric, and others nauseating.

Without noticing how, we are all back in the transport, speeding through space. "We are going to the other side of the universe," someone says. He is speaking more to my peers than to the scientists. "We have to get far enough away."

Turning to us as if to conduct a lecture, he continues, "They won't let us do this on Earth anymore. We have been planning this a long time—decades! We have been seeking out just the right place. There is no life on any planets light years from here and we will not disturb the energy patterns that have already been established. With the knowledge we gain from this, we can uncover the core secrets we were so close to before we were diverted from our efforts by the military and by war. We never finished what we started—our quest for knowledge of the universe. We want you all to see it, for you are still on Earth and you can explain what this is all about to others. You will understand why we did what we did then, before the bomb was dropped. The need for these tests will be revealed. This blast that we will undertake will be thousands of times stronger than any that happened on Earth. We will uncover the secret the universe has been hiding."

I look up into the starlit black sky and say, "How are you going to do this? I don't see enough supplies to create something like this."

"Don't worry," says a friend of my father's. "When we arrive at the edge of empty space we will use our collective minds to create a structure, like the tower at Trinity, somewhat like a linear accelerator. The result will be approximately three hundred miles high, and at the bottom we will place the collection of particles for the blast."

"We can't be so close!" I say in a panic. "Don't you remember? We will all die. Where will you be?" I scream, "Why are you doing this again?" (The reality of fear and human frailty will haunt me the next day when I awake.)

"Don't worry." This command comes from an unknown voice. "You will all be behind large, granite-like structures with special qualities. You don't have to worry about us. This cannot hurt us now."

There is a silence that lasts for what seems like an eternity, and then we arrive. The sky is smoky black, a grey mist of gases swirling out and around our craft, diamond stars showing sporadically through the darkness. The fabric of endless space is still, but alive. I look into the black hole of a shining creation that holds the mind of man searching for the mind of God.

I see inside my father's mind: all at the same time, he is in the midst of his career, starting over, finishing his dream, and searching for the secret of the universe. He is alive without the burden of the Atomic Age, without the pain of death—his own and those in Hiroshima—without the questions of his daughter giving him grief about his involvement in the bomb. Tears are pouring down my face.

Now we are there, somewhere beyond light! Our parents communicate through our minds that it is time to begin. The other children, all now middle-aged adults are dropped off behind the granite wall. We are floating, but standing upright in space. We watch a screen go up in front of our parents. We watch a tower construct itself.

"Don't!" I scream into a hollow vacuum that I watch circling down into a black hole. But it begins. We watch, and I am fascinated and panicked. I know only that moment. We watch our parents—they, who have now left Earth for the last time. We watch the energy build.

I look up. The colors are vibrant—cool indigo, smoky brown, and frothy yellow. Gases of exploding atoms swirl higher and higher, thicker and denser. Hundreds of miles past us, the tower structure explodes into a burnt-orange-colored mushroom, farther into the still emptiness of space, farther than we can see.

I hide my eyes, then look again, my nerves vibrating into the cool indigo stream of the beginnings of the explosion. My father is alive; we are all safe. I ask him in my mind, "How will you compile the data and evaluate what you have learned from this?"

"We have brought all that we need to analyze these findings," he says. "We began setting up the lab several years ago."

I don't know how much time has passed, but we hear voices in unison in our heads. "We are satisfied; it is done. We never need to do this again. Nuclear weapons and nuclear power are over. We never wanted what happened on Earth to happen. This was our goal as young physicists, our passion."

I floated, stood in space, waited a long time, and then awoke from this dream, this nightmare—the event that had been caught in the web of my heart and mind, consuming my soul since childhood.

I walked as if still in a dream through the East Bay cities and towns near San Francisco. I looked into faces I did not know. I wondered what I could say to the people I knew if I dared talk about my dream. I seemed as if I had been witness to a real event, the most powerful man-made blast—on the other side of the universe.

Eight Months Later—July 30, 2012

On a warm summer morning in the early morning light of an East Bay town, with my eyes barely open, I scan the online news reports on my desktop computer.

"Batavia, Illinois (Reuters). Physicists at a U.S. laboratory said on Monday they came tantalizingly close to proving the existence of the elusive subatomic Higgs boson—often called the 'God particle' because it may bring mass and order to the universe.

"The announcement by the Fermi National Accelerator Lab outside Chicago came two days before physicists at CERN, the European particle accelerator near Geneva, are set to unveil their own findings in the Higgs hunt. CERN houses the world's most powerful particle accelerator, the Large Hadron Collider (LHC).... The Higgs particle's presumed power to confer mass seems to endow it with the power of creation itself."[4]

I had just returned from a conference of the International Association for the Study of Dreams. At the conference, I attended many workshops and lectures that addressed the neurobiology of dreams, dream interpretation (Jungian, Freudian and others), language in dreams, and even Tarot symbolism as archetypes in dreams.

I had written down my dream in November, even though it was so powerful and felt so real that its images and details remained clear in my mind. I found the copy and printed it out. This was all a bit strange, I thought—well, more than strange. I sat and stared for a long time at what I had written.

I wondered whether the blast I had seen in my dream on the other side of the universe was real. I contemplated the possibility of my father's spirit having been at Fermi Lab eight months earlier, collaborating with the scientists who now work there. The work he had done there in the fifties on fusion—the process in which massive energy is released when light nuclei are brought together to form a heavier nucleus— had been one focus of the first Atoms for Peace conference in Geneva, Switzerland in September, 1958. Were my father and his colleagues actually able to fulfill their passion for finding the true nature of the universe?

I had asked my father one Rosh Hashanah, the Jewish New Year, when I was young how someone could be religious and a scientist. I wish I could remember what he said, because maybe that held the answer.

The news article went on: "Because the Higgs is hypothesized to exist for a mere fraction of a second before decaying into other particles, the strategy was to look for these 'daughter' particles."

I remembered my father saying, "How many times do I have to say, things are only coincidences until they are proven." Well, I thought, how would I ever prove this coincidence?

Had my father finally found not only the "daughter particles" from the Higgs boson, but his own daughter as well?

Chapter 5

Copenhagen[5]

〜

"A physicist is just an atom's way of looking at itself."
—*Niels Bohr*

I arrive early, on a cool spring evening in Berkeley, California, where flowers of every color and scent seem to always be in bloom. The director of the play greets me in the lobby of the new Berkeley Repertory Theatre. I say, "I have wanted to see this play for a decade now. I learned Danish at the age of five at a kindergarten in Denmark." I explain that the reason I spent the fifth year of my life in Copenhagen was that my father was awarded a Guggenheim Fellowship to work and study at the Niels Bohr Institute.

He says, "You are the closest connection I have heard of to this play. I hope the actors pronounce the Danish correctly!" I assure him that I only remember *hello, thank you, goodbye,* and how to count.

I walk down a narrow, dimly lit hallway to the small theater and begin to travel back to my kindergarten year, 1957-1958. For me, it was a year of snow, gardens, and gates. Behind the neighbor's house we had fun creating our own worlds that sprang into being when we went through each gated garden. The woods behind our house were called Deerhausen, where we scampered down trails we called the upper path and the downer path. The other world was my father's, the world of theoretical physics.

Ten minutes later the overhead lights flash. I choose not to sit in the front row—too close—and take a seat in the second row of the darkened room. I ready myself for subtle gestures, glances, and hidden meanings.

In front of me on stage is a brown couch—worn, comfortable, and solid. It is long enough only for two: Niels Bohr and his wife, Margrethe, or Bohr and Werner Heisenberg. Stage right are three Danish-modern-style chairs, the kind my parents brought back from Denmark in 1958 and that sat in our living room in Park Forest, Illinois, for half a century. The chairs and the couch comprise almost the entire set on stage.

The lights go out: spotlight on the director. He says a few words about the play and, as the applause dies down, a piano that had been in shadow is lit at the far end of stage left. The piano keys are moving to a Bach tune that Heisenberg's ghost plays for Bohr. In the play it is 1941, before the Manhattan Project began. Here in this living room, science, family, politics, war, and human genius collide with trust and betrayal, real and imagined.

I project myself onto the stage and back in time. The room is and is not the Bohr's living room where I sat with my family in 1957. It is now 2013 but the questions remain; some are unstated, some just raise more questions, and some are not clearly formulated for Bohr, Heisenberg, or me.

Niels Bohr and I have the same birthday, October 7. In 1957 I turned five; Niels, seventy-two. That year I was fascinated by the Chinese Pagoda at Tivoli Gardens, the lights, and the rides. Most of all I loved the Little Mermaid, the woman with fins who sat on a rock and pondered the North Sea. She never moved, just sat at the harbor staring out to sea. That year I asked my parents for a watch. They said, "When you learn to tell time you can have a watch." So I learned to tell time, in English and in Danish, and I got my first watch.

I move in my seat—the air in the theater is becoming cooler—and reach for my sweater. Heisenberg's ghost is still playing Bach. The music comes to an end, followed by applause and silence. Niels and Werner greet at the door as old friends, mentor and student, colleagues, and surrogate father and son; they greet with suspicion, warmth, and hidden agendas that will never be clearly stated. "Why has he come to Copenhagen?"[6] Margrethe Bohr asks.

Niels and Werner go for a walk, as they had done in the old days. They walk through woods with hawthorn trees I imagine I have seen before; possibly black-necked grebes are singing nearby. Light snow dusts the ground. A breeze swirls ideas in from the North Sea that has no borders, except those of the harbor and the national boundaries between Denmark and Nazi Germany. The men have not been gone long when they rush back into the house. Bohr is angry, livid; Heisenberg bolts out with formal farewells. Their friendship is forever severed.

Was Heisenberg looking for a father figure to say that he was doing the right thing, staying in Germany to develop the bomb for Hitler? Did he want Bohr to forgive him? My chair becomes more uncomfortable, the wood beneath the cushion and the armrest digs into my elbow.

Or was he trying to find out if the Americans were building the bomb and if Niels was part of that project? I wonder if Heisenberg played Bach in Bohr's living room to soothe

the pain of his own childhood from the destruction he saw in Germany during World War I and the loss of his own father. The play poses many questions, among them why he traveled in secret. He was head of the nuclear program for the Nazis, but no one knows if he purposely sabotaged the German program because of his guilt and shame. I wonder if Heisenberg said something to Bohr about his partially Jewish heritage. Despite Bohr's theory of solid-state physics, and despite Heisenberg's Uncertainty Principle,[7] nothing seemed solid.

All these questions are posed and not answered, for only he and Niels knew what happened on that short walk in the Copenhagen woods in 1941.

Why *did* he go to Copenhagen?

"Margrethe: Some questions remain long after their owners have died. Lingering like ghosts. Looking for the answers they never found in life.

Bohr: Some questions have no answers to find."[8]

Do I know something from looking wide-eyed as a child in Bohr's living room, sensing something I was never told? I often thought as a child that I experienced more than what was said. And maybe there is an answer hiding in Heisenberg's Uncertainty Principle that I will someday see like the ghosts of my childhood.

Like the ghosts of the three people being played by the actors in Copenhagen.

Chapter 6

Global Suicide

"Truth sounds paradoxical."
—*Lao Tzu*[9]

Some of my earliest memories are of having suicidal thoughts and being fatalistic; I used to spend hours pretending that I had disappeared. I wanted to get away from everything and everyone, but was afraid of truly ending it all. It was a better option to hold onto suicide as a last resort so I would always have a way out; it kept me alive, and I kept it my secret.

The reason to stay alive, however, was never quite clear to me. By pretending that I didn't exist, I could live in both worlds, fantasy and my real life, which often felt unreal. When I was about ten, I told my sister I experienced being invisible. She told me not to tell anyone, so I didn't.

I walked from one prison to another, from school to home and back. The six blocks between, I labeled "Freedom Row." I told this to my school counselor at our annual meeting to discuss my classes for the coming year at my high school— Rich East. I sat in his small office looking through the tiny window at a pile of red bricks, which seemed to embody the impenetrable wall I felt separating me from the counselor. "So next year you need English, algebra, Spanish, sociology, and, of course, gym," he said with a professional air.

I stared out the window at the spider webs and red bricks and said, "Uh huh." I looked at him, thinking he would surely see that I wanted to talk about the isolation I suffered at school and at home, that I didn't really believe that I belonged anywhere. But the school counselor just looked at me blankly. I knew he didn't have time for such unimportant personal discussions. I agreed to the list of classes and slowly walked out through the door labeled "School Counselor" as the next student entered his office.

I was glad I was in high school when Eugene McCarthy ran for president and I could enter a different world, that of politics. Door-to-door canvassing, promoting Clean Gene and peace in Vietnam, selling McCarthy blue and turquoise buttons and bumper stickers, and taking part in anti-Vietnam vigils and marches gave me a purpose. By being a part of changing the world for the better, I was also making my own life better. I rode the Illinois Central Railroad (I.C.) downtown to take art classes for high school students at the Art Institute of Chicago. I listened to Bob Dylan songs on vinyl albums spinning on my turntable until I could recite every lyric and sing every tune. "Desolation Row" was a long narrow alleyway that meandered down any lost place I would find myself. I thought I was living a line from that song with my dad as "Einstein disguised as Robin Hood with his memories in a trunk."[10] Those memories were revealed to me in unlabeled, brown-paper-wrapped photos that had been sitting in my father's closet for forty-three years.

Years later at the University of Wisconsin at Madison, I found myself standing on the top of a twenty-five story round apartment building two blocks from campus. I don't remember how I got there but do know I wanted it over and done with. The roof was where apartment dwellers went in the summer to sunbathe or have a picnic, like a flat plateau on top of a Los Alamos hill. From there I could see the entirety of Lake Mendota with its variation of blues and greens and the white and grey cumulus clouds shadowed on the water. I could see the entire twenty-five miles around the lake—the peninsulas set aside for hiking, the campus, capitol building, isthmus, and my apartment building a mile away. But I didn't focus on those sights for long. I was looking down at the cement parking lot and the piles of dead and drying yellow, brown, and red leaves. I stayed there for maybe twenty-minutes, maybe an hour, wondering if I would jump. I went back a year or so later, taking the long elevator ride to the first floor—as before—feeling partly sad, but mostly empty.

I wondered if the world was standing at my side on top of that building, round like a cyclotron, thinking of bigger and better ways to annihilate itself from another plateau with a beautiful view—Los Alamos, that also had music, picnics, and sunbathing, as well as the start of an age that would enable efficient global suicide. I believed I shared a deeply ingrained masochistic secret with an unconscious world.

Committing global suicide seemed to me like standing on that rooftop in a world driven mad by the necessity to produce—more money, more useless items, and more technology expanding to enable total destruction. Maybe the human race had a self-destructive seed that had grown to the level of mass annihilation in an instant, just as I could accomplish in one step into space. Just two nuclear weapons on either side of the world could start it all.

Maybe I just wanted company or dreamed I was Mother Earth wanting to forcibly wean the human race from the organic beauty it used to know. I thought other "children" of the Manhattan Project would be as devastated by nuclear proliferation as I was.

It seems to me there could be more than just coincidence at play here—or maybe not. Maybe when you are this fatalistic, you look for someone to share it. I was surprised to learn from my therapist many years later that most people don't spend a lot of their lives with the looming possibility of suicide as an option.

My family's connection with nuclear annihilation may have just been a convenient excuse for my not wanting to deal with living; despite that, it still seems to me that the human race has been on a path to global suicide since the technology became available with the development of the first atomic bomb. Does it matter? It did to me.

Reflecting on my childhood, I wonder if anyone really knew that I was even there. The paradox was alive inside of me, trying to disappear—but, along with being seemingly invisible to everyone around me, I wanted desperately to be seen, like the invisible atom.

I would need superpowers to make myself disappear, however, then reappear by teleportation in a different place or not at all, like the character Q in Star Trek, whom I envied. If I thought hard enough, if I projected myself, visualized myself as clear as nothing, I could have the powers of angels, twilight beings, Superman, and Superwoman.

I wanted to walk through walls and listen in on those who would do me harm. (Is this not what the world's superpowers still do as they spy on each other—and us—with ever better and more sophisticated means?)

Now I believe that my true power is in being here and using my creativity and intelligence.

During the Cold War and after, powerful nations that claimed to have nuclear weapons set out to save the world, just as Superman, the cartoon and TV hero, battled to save Metropolis from evil. At the Potsdam Conference in Germany, United States President Harry Truman, British Prime Minister Winston Churchill, and Soviet leader Joseph Stalin sat by a fireside and had a chat. Their nations each claimed to have super powers—in fact, to *be* superpowers—and they were so recognized by the world and wanted to attract other nations as allies. An illusory balance of power kept them in check through fear of retaliation.

The United States and the Soviet Union raced to build A-bombs, H-bombs, and neutron bombs, soon joined by nations all over the world. Everyone wanted in on the race. As a teenager, I remember lying on my Danish bed with its teak headboard and frame, looking at the ceiling as the turntable spun its vinyl record around and around, filling the room with Bob Dylan's nasal voice and its undercurrent of Jewish sarcasm.

"Oh my name it is nothin'
My age it means less
The country I come from
Is called the Midwest
I's taught and brought up there
The laws to abide
And that the land that I live in
Has God on its side."[11]

I still believe that every country that owns or wants to own a nuclear weapon must believe it has God on its side. That is—and always will be—a recipe for global suicide.

PART II

What Was Left Behind

Chapter 7

An Invisible Map

"Once form has been smashed, it has been smashed for good, and once a forbidden subject has been released, it has been released for good."
—Louise Bogan

A map drawn with invisible ink stretched across the United States, from the South up to the Midwest, down to the Southwest, out to the West, and up the coast to the Northwest. The locations were Oak Ridge, Tennessee; Los Alamos, New Mexico; and Hanford, Washington; along with laboratories on the University of Chicago and University of California Berkeley campuses. To anyone who did not work with the Manhattan Project those places did not officially exist.

The lines of the map were connected by the collaboration of brilliant minds, from graduate students to the top physicists and chemists they were studying under. From California, across the United States to Europe, the miles between top scientists and laboratories disappeared in the common goal of exploring the unseen world of the atom and the looming political reality of stopping Hitler. Some had escaped Nazi Germany, and some American Jewish scientists had relatives in concentration camps. The goal of the atomic-bomb project was clear and in many cases personal: a horror, with its ovens of death hidden in the barren stretches of Germany,

Poland, Austria, Latvia, Ukraine, the Netherlands, the Czech Republic, and France.

The Manhattan Project functioned as a whole, while each site made its individual contributions. The sharing of ideas, failures, and successes was critical to the Project. Prior to 1940, uranium fission had been hypothesized to be possible. Indeed it was, and on December 2, 1942, at 3:36 p.m. Enrico Fermi and his group created the world's first man-made, controlled, self-sustaining chain reaction under Stagg Field, a soccer (and former football) stadium at the University of Chicago. The success of this experiment was the first step towards the creation of the bomb.

At that exact time and day twenty-five years later, on a grassy spot just above where the reaction had taken place, a sculpture, "Nuclear Energy," was unveiled. It was added to the National Register of Historical Places on October 15, 1966, when the National Historic Preservation Act was enacted. The plaque says "On December 2, 1942 man achieved here the first self-sustaining chain reaction and thereby initiated the controlled release of nuclear energy."[12]

The sculpture has been described by some as a human skull or an atomic mushroom cloud, but Henry Moore, its sculptor, told a friend that he hoped people would "go around it, looking out through the open spaces, and that they may have a feeling of being in a cathedral." I have viewed it dozens of times and have never been quite sure what I saw or believed about it.

When my father was a twenty-three-year-old graduate student in chemistry at the University of Chicago, a friend commented matter-of-factly that he believed talking to Dr. Charles D. Coryell at the New Chemistry Building would be of interest to him. Curious about what he would discover, my father took off, wondering what fascinating concepts would unfold in that mysterious but undistinguished building on the other side of campus. He did not know that he had already been picked to be on the Project.

I imagine him briskly walking down the wide expanse of green with brown leaves and a covering of snow, down a slight hill to the depressed grass-covered flat, and across the street to the Midway, which had been designed by Frederick Law Olmsted for the 1893 World's Columbian Exposition. My father's brother, my Uncle Nate, was born that year; he was twenty-seven years older than my father and became an artist and political cartoonist supported in his early career by the Works Progress Administration (WPA). He later became a top cartoonist for the Chicago Herald. My dad went to live with Nate and his wife, Belle, at age fourteen after my grandparents passed away.

The Midway stretched through the campus, seasonally displaying a colorful mosaic of fall leaves, long months of ice and snow, and spring and summer sun-worshippers dotting the mile-long expanse flanked by 59th and 60th Streets on the South Side. Many decades later our family would enjoy leisurely picnics in the sun on a blanket laid on the freshly cut grass. But I imagine my father walking across campus that day south and east into the biting winds of Lake Michigan.

As he reached the New Chemistry Building ("New Chem," as it was referred to for many decades), I see him entering the snow and ice-crusted doors and I shiver, remembering the razor-sharp cold that I have experienced many times. I watch him walking down the long, straight hallways past the receptionist who would soon become his wife. (My mother had gotten the position with the help of her brother, my Uncle Bernard.) My father knocked on the door of Dr. Coryell's office.

I imagine a cramped office with books piled to the ceiling, a small blackboard, and a wooden desk telling its own story from years of use. I can see Dr. Coryell motioning my father to sit while he remained standing. I imagine him pacing back and forth, wild excitement lighting up his eyes, waving his arms around, and spouting calculations and theories with exuberant flights of his hands.

My father wrote in the Journal of Chemical Education: "I arrived at New Chem on an interview visit and saw a number of my former classmates and graduate assistants from the University of Chicago walking past the guard through the entrance. One of them [William (Buck) Rubinson] came out of a brief interview and then escorted me in to meet Charles Coryell in his narrow office. In his typical rapid-fire style Coryell gave the whole story of fission, radioactivity, chain-reaction piles, the scope of the project, and the race to get 'the bomb' before the Germans did. All this in less than about twenty minutes! During this tutorial outburst his shirt-tail was flapping out behind him, and he alternated between a perch on an overturned wastebasket and the blackboard to illustrate each point. Needless to say I was overwhelmed, but so caught up in his obvious deep commitment to the job and his fervor, that all I wanted to do was grab a pipet, a test tube, and a solution of bombarded uranium and get to work!"[13]

In the next twenty minutes my father's eyes were opened and his mind expanded into the realms of nuclear chemistry and the inner world of the atom. He knew the theories, but Coryell explained to him how they might be made real and put to use on a large scale. Uranium fission—the splitting of the atom—was the immediate scientific goal; stopping Hitler, the political aim of the United States and its allies.

My father's career took shape in less than half an hour after he walked through Coryell's office and a door that didn't officially exist and into the future. The principles of the unseen that he heard described in those few minutes would in a few years collide with the political realities of the world casting a global shadow over his and all our futures.

Chapter 8

Dad at Home and Work

"It doesn't matter who my father was;
it matters who I remember he was."
—Anne Sexton

My father was often in his own world, a world I barely scratched the surface of while he was alive. He had always carpooled to work at Argonne National Laboratory—"the Lab" as it was fondly referred to by the scientists—with his coworkers: fellow physicists, chemists, and engineers, some of whom had also moved to the suburbs in the fifties after working with him on the Manhattan Project. Argonne was formally chartered on July 1, 1946 to carry on the work on the Manhattan Project begun at the University of Chicago and code-named "Metallurgical Lab."

Four days a week around 7:45 a.m. a car horn honked, indicating the arrival of the carpool for the forty-five minute ride from Park Forest northwest to the lab on the edge of the southwest suburbs of Chicago.

On those days my mother had the car to grocery shop and take us to baseball games and ballet lessons. She would hand him his grey metal lunchbox; he would give her a kiss, grab his briefcase, and depending on the weather and time of year—a sweater, coat, hat, gloves, boots, or umbrella, and off he would go into his world of science. One day a week he would be the one honking in the other men's driveways.

This was the 1950s and '60s, long before carpools became ecologically and financially popular. I believe they carpooled for the time they spent together in scientific collaboration and male company as much as being able to share the car the other days with their wives. I imagine discussions I could never understand—notes and calculations passed around for them to discuss, chemical symbols and tables swirling around a blue '60s Chevy. I picture them busily writing as they passed by monotonous suburbs and cornfields. But maybe they just had "normal conversations" about their lives—what they ate for dinner, their kids' accomplishments and problems, their wives, what play they were seeing on Saturday night, or—depending on the time of year—the Chicago Cubs or Bears games.

When they reached the security gate at Argonne they showed their badges and proceeded into the lab. I envision my father in his lab coat, surrounded by equipment, chemicals, and ideas, his eyes shining, his mind far away, occupied by the most minute particles known—as vast and intricate as the universe.

At home, my father was distant. He would sit at his large teak desk in the living room, a typewriter and yellow pad in front of him. Years later, when my brother went to college, Dad sat in David's room at another teak desk. Both desks, along with most of our furniture, were brought back from Denmark when we returned from my father's year at the Niels Bohr Institute.

I knew he was thinking important thoughts, his hazel eyes with their perfect eyesight intense and engaged in his secret world. I would tiptoe around the living room and down the hallway, my eyes darting to his books, papers, and journals; but he was miles and years away—in the future or the past—but surely not there with me.

Maybe I tried to follow my father there, which may explain my chronic inability to stay in the moment. Sometimes he would explain scientific concepts and principles to me; he would talk on and on, thinking I was following what was so exciting to him, but I was soon lost in a jumbled barrage of words I did not comprehend. I always believed he would have been a great professor, lecturing his students for hours. I wish I could have understood more of what he said and that he had asked more about what was happening with me.

Sometimes he traveled to meetings in Geneva, Switzerland; Oak Ridge, Tennessee; Berkeley, California; or Los Alamos, New Mexico. When I was older, he explained his experiments at the Lawrence Berkeley Lab, like bombarding gold with various substances. His enthusiasm was evident, as it was captured in the scratchboard picture he created of part of Einstein's face fading into the universe.

I didn't know where he was then—out beyond the edges of space or deep inside the atom. Either way, I didn't get it. I was left somewhere on Earth in a 1950s suburb of ticky-tacky houses, watching my favorite shows all the way to the end in front of a black-and-white television, because there was no remote control to change the channels. My favorites— *The Twilight Zone, Superman,* and *The Fugitive,* which I always watched with my dad—seemed to sum up the times. Sometimes I felt like a vivid, multicolored fish shadowed beneath a coral reef, hiding its beauty, struggling just to survive within the darkness of the sea. Other times I was like a star, once hot at its core but now only a distant cold light that had gone out thousands of years ago.

Occasionally we would go to the cyclotron[14] at Argonne. I would try to imagine the atoms splitting. Where would they go? I wondered. I seemed to experience the power of their gigantic circles of energy within me.

I vividly remember the twelve-foot tall radiation-detection machine near the exit of the Lab that reminded me of scales in a meat-packing plant. There were two large footprints with vertical silver stripes that dwarfed our children's feet and two caverns for the hands that sucked ours in as far as our elbows to press the detector strip. Just above our heads was a huge dial indicating our radiation levels. Watching the green light come on and wondering if it was going to turn red is one of my most enduring memories of Argonne.

Once a year my family would attend the Lab picnic on the edge of Waterfall Glen Forest Preserve, which completely surrounds Argonne. There were games for the children, and the air vibrated with fun, freedom, and intellectual energy. We attended the yearly Lab musical, too, where my dad played the clarinet. I learned all the words and tunes to *Guys and Dolls, Damn Yankees,* and *South Pacific.* Sometimes we'd stay at the Lab motel in the summer and go swimming and lie in the sun. We'd look for the white fallow deer (Dama dama)[15] that roam freely inside the forest preserve on Lab property. I felt blessed each time we were lucky enough to see them.

These were times throughout my childhood when my dad's work and home life merged for me, when I felt the energy from the Lab not as the frigidity of the Cold War or the furnace of an atomic blast, but as the warmth of a family.

Chapter 9

The Graphite Pyramid

"I am prepared for the worst, but hope for the best."
—*Benjamin Disraeli*

On December 2, 1942 the Chicago Pile, constructed from graphite blocks with lumps of natural uranium, was used to create the first self-sustained nuclear chain-reaction under the west stands of the University of Chicago's football stadium. I have an illustration given to my father showing the Pile and the scientists who were gathered there that was drawn using the graphite left over from that reaction.

Inscription under the drawing:

"On December 2, 1942, man achieved the first self-sustaining controlled nuclear chain reaction in Chicago PileNumber 1 (CP-1) at the University of Chicago. This lithograph of the event is printed with ink made from graphite used in CP-1.

Leo Szilard, Athur, H. Compton, Enrico Fermi, Eugene P. Wigner."

I imagine the graphite being collected in a container like the ashes from a cremation, then opened and dipped into with brush and pen to create an artist's rendering of the event.

Natural uranium (U) is made up of more than 99% U-238, which cannot be used for a bomb. The 7/10ths of 1% that is U-235 can split, or fission, by capturing a slow neutron. This reaction produces a large amount of energy, as well as two additional neutrons that can fission two other U-235 atoms. U-235—enriched uranium—is not found in nature and is created through a process called isotope separation. It is an essential component in the development of nuclear weapons and nuclear energy.

In the winter of 1940-41, scientists at the University of California Berkeley discovered a second fissionable material, plutonium (Pu). It was not then known to occur naturally—though trace amounts would later be found in nature[16]—and was formed by the capture of a neutron by U-238. Plutonium was first synthesized in 1940 by a team led by Glenn T. Seaborg and Edwin McMillan at the Berkeley laboratory by bombarding U-238 with deuterons—the nuclei of deuterium atoms consisting of a proton and a neutron. This quickly became their lab's focus, since producing plutonium in useful quantities was essential to the Project.

"In [James Herbert] Jones Lab's Room 405, future Nobel laureate Glenn Seaborg achieved an important steppingstone on the way to the Atomic Age. [There], he weighed the first visible, pinhead-sized sample of plutonium. It wasn't much, but enough to measure its chemical and metallurgical properties."[17] [*The story of how most of that was almost lost in Los Alamos with the scientists scrambling to recover it is told in Chapter 10.*]

The industrial production chapter of plutonium began on a small scale in 1943 and was soon expanded to Hanford, Washington. The Manhattan Project continued to expand clothed in a secrecy that extended not only to the public, but to the words its participants were allowed to use with each other. Coded alphabetic and alphanumeric names identified sites of research and development of the bomb. Scattered across the United States were places simply called B, C-P1, D, F, K-25, W, X, X-10, Y, and Y-12. Site W was Hanford, Washington; Site X, Oak Ridge, Tennessee; and Project Y, Los Alamos, New Mexico.

The "town" of Los Alamos was not to be named aloud but was only referred to as The Hill. New recruits were to report to the same place where friends and families wrote to them, a nondescript post office box in Santa Fe. The upwards of three hundred thirty children who were born on The Hill during World War II had only P.O. Box 1663, Santa Fe, New Mexico listed on their birth certificates as their place of birth. Many had problems later, especially when applying for official documents.

Julie Schletter [interviewed in Chapter 19] said, "No one else in the world knew what was going on up there on the plateau—let alone that anyone was even there."

Like actors in a high-budget, reputations-at-stake project with an unfinished script, the players were under strict orders not to speak of the play or their roles. The props, the radioactive isotopes and elements, were U (uranium), U-235, U-238, and Pu (plutonium). The script itself had one plot line with one successful resolution.

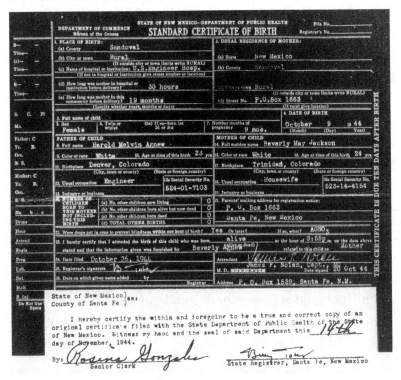

Courtesy of Los Alamos Historical Society Archives

Y-12 was a separation facility at Oak Ridge that utilized the calutron, a modification of the first cyclotron. Both the cyclotron, which was constructed at the University of California at Berkeley, and the calutron—short for California University Cyclotron—were developed by Ernest O. Lawrence based on the original concept by the German Rolf Widerøe. The calutron functioned as a mass spectrometer to separate the isotopes of uranium. At the peak of operation, there were 1,152 calutrons operating in Oak Ridge.

The second reactor, X-10, was a graphite reactor at Oak Ridge. It was 1,000 times more powerful than the first reactor—CP-1 at the University of Chicago and converted Uranium-238 into plutonium. In January 1945 the application of the radioactive isotopes it produced was diverted from weapons to science, medicine, and agriculture. In 1963 it was shut down and, in 1966, declared a National Historical Landmark.

K-25 was the Gaseous Diffusion Plant in Oak Ridge, strangely named "Happy Village." It stretched for one mile in a U-shaped, four-story building, covered two-million square feet, and at the time was the world's largest roofed structure. After World War II, K-27, K-29, K-31, and K-33 were added and produced most of the U-235 for the Cold-War weapons.

Since it was not known which uranium-isotope- separation technique—gaseous diffusion, calutron, or centrifuge— would be the most successful, General Leslie Groves insisted that all techniques be pursued simultaneously. Though not the most cost-effective strategy, it was guaranteed to result in the most rapid accumulation of U-235.

B, D, and F at Hanford were water-cooled piles six miles apart on the south bank of the Columbia River. Four separation plants, built in pairs at two sites around ten miles south of the piles, separated natural uranium (U-238) from the plutonium that was produced in the reactors.

At Los Alamos the mission was to perform research, develop technology, and produce the atomic bomb for use in the war against Germany. When work began there in 1943, construction of the site at Oak Ridge, Tennessee, had not begun, and the methods for producing a fissionable material were still theoretical. Developing these methods was a critical step.

In 1943, a separation plant based on different diffusion rates was built to produce U-235 in greater quantities than occur naturally. During the project enriched uranium had the code name "Oralloy," a shortened version of "Oak Ridge alloy."

As time went on, the military, which was in charge of the Project, interfered with the communication among the sites and among the scientists, especially between Chicago and Los Alamos. Their style of top-down, need-to-know communication did not work well with scientists. It disrupted the free flow of ideas that was critical to the success of the Project. Robert Oppenheimer, who had access to everything to do with the Project—except what the military didn't want him to know—held weekly open meetings at Los Alamos to discuss ideas, successes, and failures. But the military wanted him at the top of the pyramid with the other scientists relegated to specific assignments, so they wouldn't see the whole picture. Oppenheimer became more and more uncomfortable with the military ways.

That pyramidal, three-sided structure would be repeated in the not-too-distant future in the name of Trinity—the site where the first atomic bomb was tested—and in its memorial in a desolate landscape just outside Alamogordo, New Mexico. A pyramidal obelisk there marks Ground Zero, where the world entered the Atomic Age with the final act, testing "the gadget"—the first atomic bomb–on July 16, 1945.

The encores were Little Boy, dropped on Hiroshima on August 6, and Fat Man, dropped over Nagasaki on August 9.

The aftermath–silence.

Many roads led out of Trinity—some to the research and production of weapons that would keep the United States at the forefront of the Cold War and others to developments in peaceful uses of technology and nuclear medicine.

The advances in physics and chemistry that emerged from the successful testing of the first A-bomb opened a door not only to the secrets of the universe, but also to the problems associated with the uses of nuclear energy and the waste it produces. The confluence of human error and natural disaster have already led to disastrous accidents at nuclear power plants—Three Mile Island in 1979, Chernobyl in 1986, and Fukushima in 2011.

No one can say whether the atomic bomb would have been created without the urgency of World War II, but for anyone looking at the power available inside the nucleus, it was a small step to take. We are on a one-way historical path, however, and we do not have a time machine to go back and rearrange particles or history and tweak a few details.

What is still present is what was left behind: the aftermath of the Cold War. Despite the reduction of nuclear weapons in the world, we can still destroy any country we choose, many times over, as others can destroy the United States. According to the Arms Control Association, 15,913 warheads exist in the world.[18] The Doomsday Clock (developed by Barbara's father [Chapter 10] in 2016 reads three minutes to midnight. Including both nuclear annihilation and climate change, the clock represents how close the world is to global catastrophe.

There are several sad ironies in the development and eventual use of the atomic bomb. Accidents killed many workers during the Project. After accomplishing what the government and military asked of them, those tireless scientists and technicians who survived were rewarded with a thank you from the FBI of ongoing surveillance.

Some were watched and followed for decades. One known to everyone—Oppenheimer—was virtually destroyed. He lost his security clearance and career due to the Red Scare and the Joseph McCarthy hearings and died of throat cancer at the age of sixty-two.

The Manhattan Project was ultimately a frightening success. The scientists' achievements were so overwhelming that members of the government and military who had desperately wanted them to succeed became afraid of them. This left some scientists appalled at what they had created and incensed at the very powers that had encouraged and supported the Project.

Academic science and research programs had been co-opted by the subsequent production of the H-bomb, the neutron bomb, and the stockpiling of all nuclear weapons—in the duplicitous name of the "security" of the nation.

Protest was alive, however, and petitions called for demonstrations of these weapons before their use and for President Truman not to drop the bomb. In 1953 President Eisenhower gave a speech to the United Nations about the peaceful use of atomic energy. In 1955 and 1958 the first and second Atoms for Peace conferences were held in Geneva, Switzerland. Five thousand scientists and government officials came together to discuss the applications of nuclear energy for peaceful purposes.

During the war scientists were excited to be searching for the secrets to the universe while at the same time finding a way to stop Hitler. They were instrumental in eventually ending the Second World War. But the failure of that success haunts our world to this day.

PART III

Talking with Other "Children"

Chapter 10

Barbara Englar M.

≈

Barbara saw my ad on the Atomic Heritage Foundation website (www.atomicheritage.org) and agreed to talk with me about her memories of her father, Kenneth Englar, a chemical engineer who was assigned to Los Alamos while in the U.S. Army. Barbara is married to a Japanese-American man whose mother was living in Japan when the bomb was dropped.

The story of Kenneth Englar's arrival at Los Alamos was one I was to hear many times: a brief letter, no details, just instructions to go to a nondescript post office box in a nondescript Santa Fe post office.

No one who received this letter to appear there knew what was going to happen when he or she arrived. At the post office there were instructions to proceed to 109 East Palace in Santa Fe. Once there, Dorothy McKibbin, Oppenheimer's secretary and assistant, greeted them and arranged the proper credentials, paperwork, and badges; they were promptly whisked away to a stunning location—a landscape Oppenheimer had fallen in love with in his youth when he was sent there by his father to recover after contracting colitis on a family trip to Europe.

Traveling down a gravel back road through the desert and up a harrowing drive to the top of a plateau, the new arrivals soon found themselves in a world of brilliance and

*poorly built housing guarded by the military. The land-
scape was filled with 50,000-to-60,000-year-old volcanic
pumice from nearby Redondo Peak. There were strange
and colorful plants and shrubs, huge desert boulders, and
plateaus rising from the barren floor. They named their
isolated high desert retreat Los Alamos, Spanish for "pop-
lar trees", code name "The Hill," but all their friends and
families back home knew was the P.O. Box in Santa Fe.*

In December of 1943 my father graduated from Columbia
University in an accelerated three-year program with a chemical engineering degree. He was drafted into the Army in 1944
and ended up going through basic training three times due
to a plan, unknown to him, to have him transferred to New
Mexico instead of being sent overseas. He was relieved to find
out he wasn't a failure as a solider.

An Army captain he met in college was stationed in Los
Alamos and had worked behind the scenes to have him transferred. All the paperwork and the approvals for the transfer
were top secret, which is why it took so long. He was the only
person in his Army unit who went to New Mexico.

He received his orders, early in 1945, to report to P.O.
Box 1663, Santa Fe, New Mexico—no instructions on where
it was or what to do when he arrived there. He says in his
memoirs that he envisioned standing in a post office, staring
at a wall.

*Off to some P.O. Box in Santa Fe, inside the box you go
for the remainder of the war.*

My dad wrote of the striking terrain, a dramatic contrast

from New York City where he had spent his entire life. He had taken his time traveling across the country by train and was late arriving in Santa Fe. He arrived on The Hill with Dorothy [McKibben] and was surprised he was expected at a certain time. He was immediately yelled at by the sergeant. His previous experience with the Army had been that every time he was transferred and his unit arrived, nobody had any idea what they should be doing or that they should even be there. Based on this, he didn't see any reason to rush around.

The major said if this had been the real Army he would have put him in the brig. Here there was no marching, no physical conditioning, no saluting, no KP duty, no latrine duty, and no curfew. He thought that was pretty great compared to his three basic trainings.

My father was surprised to find out there were new manmade elements he had never heard of. In school he had learned that there were ninety-three elements; now he found out there was a secret element, plutonium—number 94— known only to those on The Hill and in other secret facilities around the country. He was amazed and awed to be working with scientists who had developed a new element[19] (especially Art Wahl, one of the co-discoverers of plutonium).

One of his coworkers told him he had been trying to work on the Harvard cyclotron, as part of his Ph.D. studies, and that it was always down for maintenance, so he gave up on his research. When my dad arrived at Los Alamos, the cyclotron was there. They had moved it in secret. No one at Harvard knew what had happened to it. He wrote in his journal: "I discovered secret negotiations had taken place between Harvard President James B. Conant and General Groves to sell the cyclotron for $1 to the government with the promise of a new cyclotron at Harvard after the war." They kept their promise. The story that was told to everyone else was that it was needed for medical research for military personnel. I don't think he had ever worked with radioactive materials before.

Was he purifying plutonium?

Yes, the first atom bomb was a uranium core, the second bomb was plutonium. Uranium was the heaviest of the elements and was more available.

I remember when I was about nine, my father gave me a pamphlet to read about uranium mining. I can still see the glossy picture on the cover: a deep pit, a mine, dark and mysterious. It seemed intriguing but I didn't understand at the time what uranium was used for. I remember thinking that it was something very important to my father, but was not very interested in it. When I was older I thought it strange he had given me the pamphlet, but maybe he was just trying to get me interested in what he did.

One time my dad spilled plutonium on his bare hand. Even though they had these precautions, they weren't always using them properly. I'll read you exactly what he wrote:

"One time I foolishly spilled a test tube on my hand. I held up my hand to the Geiger counter and [the] reading was extremely high. A friend who was a good chemist had me scrub my hands with potassium permanganate crystals. He repeatedly had me scrub my hands with the crystals to reduce the speed at which the Geiger counter reacted. It took several weeks of scrubbing before the radiation count got dropped to a reasonable level.

Those of us who worked with plutonium were given a three-day pass every month and were removed from possible sources of radiation. When we came back our urine was collected. After one of those three-day passes I was found to have a small amount of plutonium in my urine and I joined an exclusive club of Hill residents called the UPPU Club... For those of you who are not current on symbols or may have forgotten that the symbol for plutonium is PU, you can now figure out the rest. There were twenty-six members who were followed for fifty years."

I don't even know if the potassium permanganate crystals are available anymore.

Potassium permanganate crystals, I thought, making a mental note. "I'll remember that, just in case," I said aloud with a degree of fear of the future. You never know.

He received boxes in the mail to send off samples of different bodily fluids and Los Alamos would test them. My mother was a nurse and was very supportive of the research that was done to study these men. Later I thought that every five years was not often enough.

Once a year would definitely have made more sense.

My dad was very low-key about the whole experience. Sometimes in school we would read about the effects of radioactivity and I thought, oh my God, it could melt your hand. It was surprising to me that he had been in contact with radioactive materials and was able to talk about it firsthand. Nobody else I knew could do that.

Did it burn?

He never said. In the beginning of his memoir he talked about a plutonium solution, so it might not have been purified yet.

He told about the time one of his coworkers, Jim Gergen, was purifying plutonium and dropped the test tube that contained much of the free world's plutonium on the floor of D Building. It was obviously too valuable to lose, so the linoleum floor covering was taken out and they devised an ad hoc chemical extraction project to recover as much plutonium as possible.[20]

How horrible. I can't imagine how they must have felt when all of the plutonium they knew about in the world was lying on the floor. [There was a long pause as we both reflected on this occurrence, then Barbara continued.]

I know. Probably just another one of those moments that happened during the Project.

The amount of plutonium in the world was meager, not enough to permit much experimentation. One of the men at the lab developed chemical methods to deal with microscopic amounts of plutonium. They wanted it purified because plutonium in its purest form would work most efficiently in the bomb and would not interfere with the nuclear reaction in the final bomb material. He was in the lab where they were working with a very small amount of plutonium. They had to purify it with state-of-the-art equipment at the time. They had glass cylinders and stainless-steel Teflon gaskets because they wanted materials it wouldn't react with. All the materials used in purification had to be chemically inert. They used Teflon which, back then, was a secret material.

Glen, another man I met at the Manhattan Project

reunion, told me they developed Teflon for work on the bomb.

I didn't know that. Well, of course, Teflon didn't react with anything. Key processes used to separate the impurities from plutonium [were themselves] dangerous, so workbenches had special ventilation systems.

Even as the chemical reactions were being developed, there was a remote site where all the plutonium was to be purified before it was converted to metallic plutonium [in a plant] that was being built on one of the nearby mesas. So they helped design and install the purification equipment and when it was completed, my dad was one of the GIs who operated the facility.

What did your father do after the war?

The first thing he did was write a letter to his [parents and sister] around August 7, 1945, just after the war ended. He was excited to finally share with his family what he had been doing. They had been allowed to send letters, but any sensitive information was censored. He typed: "After such an awfully long period of secrecy, it's wonderful to be able to act like normal human beings again." He continued as he learned the extent of the damage from the first bomb [dropped on Hiroshima]: "...the loss of lives as a result of the explosion was more than 150,000—or more than the total number of lives lost by the American Army, Navy, and Marines in the First World War. It seems that the world has finally reached the stage where it will be far too costly to wage war. I think that we are finally able to say that there will be no future wars— either for fear of using atomic-powered bombs, or, if they are used, there will be no war fought after that one. There won't be people enough to fight one. It's a wonderful and, at the same time, a terrifying thought."

I wish he had been right when he said, "there will be no future wars."

After the project was over he stayed on at Los Alamos a bit longer. But he had to find a job. He was discharged from the army when the war ended and returned to Los Alamos as a civilian. He tried to find a job, but there weren't many opportunities. After nine months of civilian life on The Hill it became apparent there wasn't anything as exciting as there had been to help end the war. Many technical people left to return to familiar places and a more normal life. He really liked the area though. His parents had moved to California, and he found a job there working for Douglas Aircraft [*which later became McDonnell Douglas before it became part of Boeing*] in the aerospace business. Before that he worked for a while at the Jet Propulsion Laboratory (JPL) in Pasadena.

One year we went out to Los Alamos for a vacation and he was given a thorough exam. They were trying to follow up on all the people who had that initial plutonium exposure— the UPPU club. He said even after the fifty-year study they found they were healthier than the norm. As far as I know he didn't have any lasting effects.

That's wonderful! [But I was surprised, knowing that many people from the different sites developed cancers in various organs of the body, including the brain, colon, and pancreas, which took my father's life. Many of these cancers were later confirmed by the Department of Labor as having a direct correlation to their work on the Project.]

Did your father ever share how he thought and felt about his work on the Project and the aftermath of Hiroshima? A number of people I talked to, including my father and uncle, didn't discuss it much. As a matter of fact, I didn't even know that my uncle had worked on the H-bomb until recently.

If we asked him, he would talk about it. I never met anybody else growing up whose parent had worked on the atom bomb during World War II. Many of my friends' fathers had been in World War II, but were overseas. I thought it was quite unusual to have a parent who worked on the Project.

I agree.

My dad saved pieces from the remains of an A-bomb test at Alamogordo. It became known as a new manmade mineral—trinitite—the sand beneath the tower that turned into a green glass substance.

Dana brought some with him to the reunion that his father collected after the test. I joked to him about having radioactive materials on the plane and that it was amazing they let him through security. I have a photograph of him standing next to a sign when we went to New Mexico, warning about taking any trinitite out of the area.

My dad let me take some of the trinitite to show to my high school chemistry class. We held it up to the Geiger counter and it still had traces of radioactivity. I thought that was a bit strange that he let me take it to school.

Yes, a bit odd. My father had some of the trinitite that he "won." My brother, David, told me recently that they had contests at all the sites to estimate the yield of the Trinity blast, and my father came closest at Chicago. David still has some pieces of it.

How did your Dad get the trinitite? Did he go out to the site afterwards?

One his buddies went; he wanted to watch the test and

it was still secret. He said he was going to go "fishin'," a play on the word "fission," the actual explosion.

Scientists' humor.

When his buddy returned from the test, another friend asked how was the fishin', and then he realized that his question could have been determined to violate security.

Did your father know beforehand they were going to drop the bomb?

I don't know if they knew when it was going to be dropped; they might have been told right before. By then Germany had surrendered.

That was the whole reason for the petition to Truman to not use it on Japan, because the war was over in Germany. I think once the test was successful, it was a foregone conclusion.

But they were not completely confident that the bomb would work.

Right, they had only tested the one and it was in a stationary man-made tower in the desert. The weather was a factor when they had to drop it out of a plane, which is why they changed the second site from Kokura to Nagasaki.

In a way it was kind of amazing that it did work, I guess, unfortunately.

There is a pamphlet I found at a garage sale one time. It was the bible regarding atomic attacks.

Someone else I talked to found a copy in her father's belongings.

It's very disturbing; this booklet states a pretense that you can survive. It says, "You can survive, you can live through an atomic bomb raid, and you won't have to have a Geiger counter. You won't have to wear protective clothing or have any special training in order to do it." It goes on to explain that the bomb is not too dangerous and the steps you can take to escape it. I found this very disturbing. I think there is not enough awareness in today's world and exactly how dangerous, lethal, and unnecessary nuclear weapons really are. I think we should get rid of them. We need to solve our...

...problems other ways.

I completely agree.

Do you know what year it was published?

October 1950. The office of Civil Defense in California distributed it. It's so ridiculous; it goes on and on; it's thirty pages long. All the tips on what to do and how to survive and, don't worry, it's just a bomb! It's pretty bizarre. The pamphlet says, "Kill the myth; atomic weapons will not destroy the earth."[21]

I feel better already.

It continues, "While an atom bomb holds more death and destruction than man has ever before wrapped in a single package, its total power is definitely limited.... Naturally, your chances of being injured are far greater than your chances of being killed. But even injury by radioactivity does not mean that you will be left a cripple, or doomed to die an early death. Your chances of making a complete recovery are much the same as for everyday accidents."[22] A little cheery, happy little face; it may ruin your day but...

Then came the duck-and-cover campaign.

I remember in elementary school we learned to read and write and drop under our desks, and make sure to cover our heads. I remember even as a kid thinking that I'm hiding under this cute little desk with little metal legs, hands over my head, and is this really going to protect me if an atom bomb is dropped on the playground? I don't think so!

[Laughter.]

It was ridiculous.

Maybe we can get some tidbits about surviving a nuclear war.

It's not that hard, a walk in the park.

My cousin Daniel told me his dad told him, "If there is a bomb dropped on Chicago we're all going to be dead, so don't even worry about it." Do you know if your dad has any old pictures from Los Alamos?

I think he has a copy of a paper, *The Santa Fe,* a New Mexico newspaper, which devoted the whole first page to the story of Los Alamos. It put to bed the rumors of what was going on up there, such as a submarine being built and a tunnel that was going to stretch out to the ocean.

In the middle of the desert? Well, I suppose they would have never guessed the truth. Do you remember some of the questions you asked your dad?

I think I asked him at the time whether they knew what they were doing. Of course, it was all secret and they didn't know what they were supposed to be doing until they arrived at Los Alamos.

I asked him how he felt that the A-bomb was dropped on a civilian population. At the time he said he thought it prevented more death. My dad's a quiet person, so I don't really know if it bothered him, or if it stills bothers him. At the time he had no choice once he was there. My dad was never a supporter of any war. I don't know if that was a result of his experience at Los Alamos. We never had guns or any kind of weapons in the house. We never even had that much high tech around the house. My dad, working in aerospace, would say he had high-tech, state-of-the-art equipment at work but didn't want [it] at home.

Did he work with Oppenheimer?

My dad only saw Oppenheimer a few times. He said what made the biggest impression on him about Oppenheimer was that he was continuously running all over the country to the various sites of the Project. He drove around in his old beat-up car, wore old holey sweaters, didn't dress like an executive, didn't have fancy clothes, and was very down to earth. He said he was approachable and didn't seem to care what he looked like or what he was wearing. I think that really stuck with my dad; he had never been very impressed with people who were impressed with the way people looked. He said none of the scientists really cared what they looked like.

That's true. My father had a favorite old plaid red-and-black plaid flannel shirt. It was an anti-fashion statement for me to wear my favorite—his light blue, denim-type shirt over my t-shirt.

Do you have siblings?

Yes, I have two older brothers and a younger sister.

Have you ever talked with them about your dad's work and how they felt about it?

Not at length. It didn't really come up much when we were growing up. My dad was very busy with his career. We were all busy with our own interests, and my dad never lived in the past. He was always involved in the present.

When my brothers were teenagers in high school and the Vietnam War was going on, there was a possibility that they would be drafted. It was a large concern to my parents. There was no encouragement for my brothers to go into the army—just the opposite.

Mine either! My brother had to report to the draft board because he had a low number in the lottery. I told my dad I was going to take the car and drive my brother to Canada. He wasn't accepted due to allergies and a bad knee, but it was a close call. The last doctor on the board rejected him. Of course, I was sixteen and my father and brother never said anything about Canada.

You said you didn't know anybody else whose parents worked on radioactivity or the Project. As for me, I felt there was something about our family that was different—that there was something we were not supposed to talk about, whatever that difference was. It was an unspoken rule and very confusing. Because my father and my uncle both worked on the project, my cousins were all included in this secretive extended family, so this concept was magnified. There was this place apart that was our world. Did you experience any of this separateness?

I believed there was a difference: there was no one else I could compare notes with who had any type of similar experience. If we talked to other people, they thought it was interesting, but that's as far as it went. My dad didn't keep it a secret; he said he would tell people if they asked, "I was just a grunt purifying plutonium."

Just a grunt [I said with surprise]? He had a very important job.

He looked at it as being just a technical job. My dad worked on some other top-secret projects at Douglas Aircraft and other projects that were not top secret, but we never really knew what he was doing. He never took us to work; about once a year the company would have people come to visit. They would put away all the classified materials. He definitely liked to keep his work life separate from his private life.

We didn't know exactly what he did. I do know one of the last things he did at McDonnell Douglas. Right before he retired, he said, "I can't tell you what I am doing, but after it's over I can tell you." He was involved in SDI, the "Star Wars" project.

My father worked on that as well, at Argonne Lab. Later in his career he was director of the Chemistry Division at Argonne and he was going back and forth to Washington to negotiate with the politicians for funding for SDI—which he absolutely hated.

Did he encourage any of you to go into science?

Somewhat. My sister and I were more serious students than our brothers, and my dad said that companies needed women engineers for equal opportunity. When I was in college I didn't know what to major in so I took an Introduction to Engineering class. There were two other women in the class [whom] I was friends with; their fathers were also engineers and they were also told they should check out engineering as a career.

The instructor was kind of a male chauvinist who sometimes singled us out and made us feel very uncomfortable. I thought that I didn't want to have to deal with that attitude and having to prove myself over and over again.

That doesn't sound comfortable or encouraging at all.

Because of that mentality I didn't pursue engineering. My dad also encouraged my sister, and she got a degree in physics and became a high school teacher. She would have been a good engineer too, but for whatever reason she didn't want to do that.

We grew up, though, with an appreciation of science of all kinds. Both my parents had degrees in science—my father, chemical engineering and aerospace; my mother, an R.N.— and shared with us the impact of science on our daily lives, in little ways, such as gardening and even cooking, and in larger ways, like watching rocket launches and touring a mock-up of the International Space Station when it was still in the planning stages.

Seeing the space station, that sounds exciting! What field did you go into?

I studied environmental design, which combines art and a bit of science. My husband is an engineer, [and] our son, a nephew, and a niece all got degrees in engineering. It runs in the family.

You said you are married to a Japanese man?

Japanese-American, so maybe I think about the atomic bombs more than some people. I did some research about why the United States chose a civilian target. I don't know exactly why that was chosen. I guess they wanted an impact that would show the most damage.

I agree. That was a large population and they figured if they dropped the first bomb, there would be an immediate surrender but that obviously didn't happen. They still didn't surrender until five days after the second bomb dropped on

Nagasaki.

I was curious about that decision and looked for more information in my dad's memoirs. My dad mentioned General Groves. He was a character, and I guess some of the scientists and technical people didn't think much of him. In retrospect, he enabled a lot of the funding and support to do the work for the Project. He made some important contributions but it seems that some of the people thought he took too much credit. He had some influence in the decision that [the bomb] was dropped on a civilian population and not a military target.

Truman had the final decision. There were orders for the Japanese soldiers to kill all the POWs in the Philippines; he and many others believed the bomb saved their lives.

They believed they were forgotten. At least it did end the war; at that point it didn't look like it would have ended very soon. I think my parents were just glad when the war was over.

You mentioned that you were in Los Alamos once?

Yes, when we were kids, my dad had to go there for a physical exam. He took my sister and me; my brothers were teenagers and they weren't interested in going. My dad rented a motor home and we drove out in the summer. It was really hot. I don't remember much when we got there, just that he had to take a lot of medical tests. He didn't talk much about it; I didn't understand why he was taking part in those medical tests until I was an adult. I believe he didn't want to worry us. I remember he told us about some underground building or bunker that was specially constructed to test for radioactivity. He would go in there and they could conduct specialized tests to see if he had any residual radioactivity.

What are your personal views on your family's relationship to nuclear weapons?

I found this speech Eisenhower gave to the American Society of Newspaper Editors in April of 1953 which was eloquent and sums up my beliefs:

"Every gun that is made, every warship launched, every rocket fired signifies, in the final sense, a theft from those who hunger and are not fed, those who are cold and are not clothed. This world in arms is not spending money alone. It is spending the sweat of its laborers, the genius of its scientists, the hopes of its children. The cost of one modern heavy bomber is this: a modern brick school in more than thirty cities. It is two electric power plants, each serving a town of 60,000 population. It is two fine, fully equipped hospitals. It is some fifty miles of concrete pavement. We pay for a single fighter with a half-million bushels of wheat. We pay for a single destroyer with new homes that could have housed more than 8,000 people. This is not a way of life at all, in any true sense. Under the cloud of threatening war, it is humanity hanging from a cross of iron."[23]

I thought that quote was so true; if you are investing in war you're not investing in the good things to benefit the world. From my dad I thought that all the scientists at Los Alamos were brilliant, they all worked together so beautifully, and they did something that no one thought could ever be done, especially in the amount of time they had—and yet, what was the result? That was the tragedy of it all!

Exactly.

If you had that coordinated effort again it would be incredible. It's been sad in many ways. There are a lot of brilliant, very dedicated people in science and also in the military. My dad said he met some really sharp guys in the military. It would be wonderful to have projects that benefited the world.

Yes, I know. One of the things my father said was, they were scientists and researchers and they hoped that good things were done with their discoveries. I projected that he felt if they did their job right, their discoveries could be used for good-nuclear medicine for one, but most of the research at the National labs went toward continuing to develop nuclear weapons.

I do think there is a responsibility for their discoveries, and many scientists carried that burden with them. After the war if they continued in research, like my father, they were stuck in a world of being funded by the government, which wanted to build more weapons and continue the Cold War.

Have you ever been to Japan?

Yes, we have visited Japan twice. My husband still has relatives there so we got to see them and different parts of the country. We did not visit the southern part yet, so we have not been to Hiroshima or Nagasaki.

What does your husband think about the bomb and its being dropped on Japan? Did his parents come from Japan?

It is still difficult to get information from them concerning their reaction to the bombs being dropped. I don't speak Japanese but, even if I did, it is not something they want to discuss. My husband's mother was living in a town near Tokyo, far from the atomic bomb blasts, but fairly close to other attacks during WWII. She talked about having a bomb shelter built in their house outside of Tokyo.

She said when the U.S. invaded Afghanistan and the Taliban intimidated the people, it must have been similar to what it was like living in Japan during World War II. The military ruled and it was extremely oppressive. Her family had a barbershop, and if a solider came in and wanted a haircut, whoever was sitting in the chair had to jump up and move out of the way. Whatever the soldiers wanted had to be done; the military called all the shots in Japan and had brainwashed the leaders. She said later, if she knew then what she knows now, she would have realized attacking the United States was ridiculous. She is happy to be living in the U.S.

My husband's father's family [was] interned in the United States, but they had relatives near Hiroshima. We were told that he visited that family during the war, but now those details are hazy. Too many relatives have passed and no one left detailed accounts. It was a very painful time for my husband's relatives who were American citizens—born in the U.S.—but then interned. My husband's relatives living in Japan were under military rule during the war, and it was very difficult for them as well.

Many Japanese families didn't support the war, but they had no choice. In many of the Japanese movies the sons would go off to war, and the parents didn't want to send them. It's different than the image you get in the U.S. that all the Japanese just wanted war. It was the military; they were the ones who wanted it.

Then all those innocent civilians were killed.

That's what is happening again now in other countries.

Exactly.

How do you see the future?

Some days I'm optimistic and others days very concerned. I'm not sure we are learning our lessons.

I don't think so.

What really bothers me is that the United States probably has more weapons of mass destruction than any other country in the world, and there's a lot of hypocrisy about that and a lot of misleading our country, our citizens, about what we have.

I agree. Anything else you would like to add?

I think it is important for everyone to recognize the contribution of science and scientists to our daily lives and appreciate the detailed process involved in these achievements. On a personal level, even though the relatives on both sides of our family were living in countries that were at war with each other in the 1940s, we couldn't have asked for a more caring family, especially to our two sons. Both sets of grandparents adored our kids and were great friends to each other. Although my husband's father died before I met my husband, his mom is still around! We were able to take both of our sons to Japan in 2007, and they met their relatives. It was wonderful. My hope is that small steps like that will help pave larger pathways to peace in the future.

Chapter 11

Ruby Nelson

❧

*Ruby, a United Methodist pastor from Beaumont, Texas,
grew up an only child on a farm outside of Giddings,
Texas. Her father, E. Robert Beckendorf, was a sergeant
in the Army assigned to work closely with the Corps of
Engineers. As a carpenter and cabinetmaker, he helped
build the tower that held the bomb at the Trinity site. We
connected through my ad on the Manhattan Project website. She preferred to write out her answers to give her time
to think before responding, so I sent her a questionnaire I
had prepared and received her responses a few weeks later.
My written questions began by asking Ruby whether her
father had discussed his work with her.*

❧

Are there specific stories you remember?

I was in junior high school when I became aware of my
father's involvement with the Manhattan Project and thought
it was very exciting he had been involved with something so
important. The bomb itself, however, was not a topic of discussion. When I was older, I became saddened by the long-lasting
effects that the experience had on him.

My father talked about his work starting around 1960.
I think, before then, he was still concerned that he was

under security surveillance. He told me what it was like to be assigned to a base where they had to live under tight procedures and laws. All letters to and from my father were read before being sent.

One of my aunts remembers going to see my father while he was stationed at White Sands. My aunt noticed a man who always seemed to be at the same place she was. When she got on the train to go home, he spoke to her: "Have a good trip home, Miss Beckendorf." It was then that she realized she had been under surveillance the whole time she was visiting my father. She and my father always assumed that it was the FBI.

Much later, after the war, a man rented a room at my grandmother's. One evening the man appeared to be drunk and tried to get my father to talk about his experiences during the war. My father, who did not drink, did not take the bait. At one point the man's wallet fell off of the table, and it opened to his FBI identification. My father always laughed about the man's instant sobriety and apology.

My father was a high-school dropout, was drafted, and yet he ended up sitting in some high-security meetings with internationally known scientists. He heard the stories about how the bomb could cause global destruction. He was very honored by the amount of trust the military had in him but overwhelmed by the knowledge of what he was a part of. I know that my father's involvement was not by choice.

What he did mention was what happened to prepare for Trinity. My father worked on the structure that held the bomb. There wasn't much in his memoirs about what specifically he did there, but he was in a military hospital after the first test.

Why was he in the hospital? Was there a spill?

He told me that he knew when and where the test was to be done, so he made sure that he was in a location to see the explosion when it happened. Late in his life he indicated to me that his hospitalization was as much psychological as it was physical. Even though his involvement with the testing was involuntary, he was still very troubled that he had played a part in it.

As I grew older, I felt great sadness that my father had been through the trauma of working on the atomic bomb project, not to mention the experience of being under security surveillance for several years thence.

Did he ever discuss with you and your family how he felt about the bomb being dropped on Japan?

The bombing of Japan was never mentioned. I don't know why. It wasn't until I was almost grown before I associated the White Sands testing site at Trinity with Hiroshima and Nagasaki. My suspicion is that it was too close to my father. My mother was not inclined to discuss such things. She was too busy milking cows and gathering eggs.

I was born after the war and was reared during the Cold-War era. My association was the threat of the Soviet Union dropping an atomic bomb on us. Then there was the Cuban Bay of Pigs fiasco when there were supposedly atomic weapons aimed at the United States. I clearly remember seeing the films about what to do in case of a bomb. It's almost funny now, because I realize how futile any protective measures would have been. I found an almost cartoon-like booklet put out by the National Defense Office in my father's papers, "How to Prepare for A Nuclear Attack." It was quite amusing.

Do you know your parents' views on the bomb being

dropped?

My father was always sensitive to loud noises. That may just be a personality trait, since I have the same thing. However, the onset of sonic booms in the sixties really set his nerves on edge. Our house was in the path of some flight testing out of a San Antonio Air Force base. He knew what the sonic booms were, but they brought back old fears and memories. They drove the poor chickens crazy, too.

Do you believe your father's involvement affected your outlook on the world?

My father's involvement made me more aware of man's inhumanity to man and the lengths that we will go to kill each other.

What are your political views?

I am much more socially liberal than my parents were. Ironically, I do not remember either of my parents ever voting, and I am at the polls every time. It's a baby-boomer thing.

As a clergywoman I am very careful not to publicly align myself with one political party over another. However, I was able to express my opinion on some political issues. I have preached against capital punishment. I have participated in campaigns to encourage the Texas legislature to reinstate medical coverage for children in poverty. I have also written and preached on the dangers of school-sponsored prayer in public schools.

Do you know what your father's views were?

My father definitely distrusted the government. I understand that he did some volunteer campaign work for Dwight Eisenhower—beyond that, nothing. In part this was because of the secretive nature of the work that he had been involved in.

Ironically, my father's mistrust of the government did not take root in me. I worked for the government for twenty-three years. Even though I understand something of the impersonal, awkward inefficiency of government, I do not see the government as an enemy. I see the government as a tool to implement the wishes of the American people.

As a youngster I knew that I wanted to be in a career that directly benefited people. I worked as a case manager for the State of Texas for twenty-three years. Being a United Methodist pastor is my second career.

What are your views on nuclear energy?

I have mixed thoughts about nuclear energy. I don't know enough about the dangers of it to make any statement. A member of my church works in nuclear medicine. I never realized how much that is used, but believe that is positive. As far as the bomb, I see it as just one more way for people to control and kill each other.

How would you describe your goals?

Personally, to leave the world in a little better shape than I found it. Professionally, I have a second career, as is typical of baby boomers.

There was a pervasive silence that covered the Project and discussion of it. Do you see that carrying over to your life in some way?

I'm assuming that you mean silence as compared to discussion. I have a social-worker background and I have an appreciation for bringing concerns to light so they can be disarmed.

Do you believe dropping the bomb was the right thing?

I'm not sure, nor am I sure about my views on nuclear energy. But for the foreseeable future, it is too much of a political hot potato for development. This is Texas, and many here believe there is adequate oil underground. I wish solar energy would be expanded in research and use.

How do you think people will look at the bomb's place in history in one hundred years?

I think it will be looked upon as a desperate attempt for control and power. I *hope* [Ruby's emphasis] the effect of the nuclear bomb is to remind us of how vulnerable we all are. I also hope that the memory of the bomb will put the brakes on the development of further weapons of mass destruction.

What are your views globally concerning the future?

What goes around comes around. In some ways the more things change, the more they stay the same. My parents' views were a little more pessimistic than mine on the future.

I would have to agree with that about my parents' views, but then I don't really know. I can't ask now. My mother felt very afraid from growing up during the Holocaust. I am pretty fatalistic. At least they had the optimism to bring children into the world and believe in the promise of America. Do you have children?

Yes, two adopted children. There is an interesting story about my granddaughter, who was asked a couple years ago to interview a veteran as part of a Veterans Day assignment in school. She couldn't find a veteran to interview, so my daughter told her about my father's work on the atomic bomb. The next day my granddaughter told the story to her fifth-grade class. My granddaughter never knew her great-grandfather, but now she knows the story.

Do you see the future of the world as opportunity or futility?

Opportunity. I know enough about the history of the world to know that there are ups and downs, and sometimes, what appears to be one is actually the other.

How has the "the bomb" played or not played a role in the shaping of your views on the world?

Maybe it's because I was born after the war, but there are other world events that more affect my world-view than the bomb. Events like the civil-rights movement(s) have had a stronger effect on me.

Fueled by the anti-establishment political ideals of the sixties, the backlash against technology, and the back- to-the-land sentiment, I began to distrust those in power more and more. Slogans such as "Question authority" and "If you're not part of the solution, you're part of the problem" inspired me to create my own grim mantra: "Maybe it's better to not succeed." My personal fear of success reflected from me to my view of the world and back, leaving me with little hope for the future—for myself, or for the world.

As a child of the sixties I, too, had a bit of anti-establishment in me. At one time I had a plaque that said "Never trust anyone over thirty" hanging in my bathroom. When my ex-husband turned thirty, I offered to take it down. He suggested that we leave it up as a reminder to ourselves to be true to our beliefs. The ex-husband is gone and the plaque is long gone, but the memory abides.

What stood out as the most memorable conversations you had with your father?

The time my father told me that I am a miracle child.

He and my mother did not think they could have children. My father came down with the mumps while in basic training. His superiors ordered him to continue training until he passed out from fever. Severe mumps in adult men can result in sterility. A few years later I came along.

For many years I was a member of a Radical-Therapy group that believed that only through challenging and changing a person's inner world would the political and outer world be able to grow and change, and also that only by changing the outside and political worlds would any inner growth and changes be supported and maintained. What do you think about these ideas?

I agree completely with the first part. In fact, it is consistent with the Christian gospel. I grew up with occasional attendance at church; we were Christians. I am now a United Methodist pastor, as is my husband. I am less sure about the second part. I would like to think that my strength is not that dependent on external forces.

What do you fear the most?

A society that has no concern for human dignity and human life.

What do you most value in the world?

The times when God's Kingdom breaks through—don't forget I'm a pastor. We always talk like that.

[Ruby ended this interview with a quote from the Bible and a summation of her view of the people who worked on the Project:]

Numbers 14:18 says, "[The Lord] does not leave the guilty unpunished; He punishes the children of the fathers to the third and fourth generation." That's not an indictment of the men and women who planned and carried out the Manhattan Project. They did what they felt they had to do. It does refer to the constant human search for ways to destroy each other and how that search affects generations to come.

Chapter 12

Robert Lawrence

～

A member of my writing group mentioned that he had worked as a pathologist with Robert Lawrence, son of Ernest O. Lawrence, who invented the cyclotron and was among the top group of scientists on the Manhattan Project. Robert was named after Robert Oppenheimer and lives in the San Francisco area. We spoke in 2010.

～

My mother was Molly Lawrence; her first name was Mary, but everyone called her Molly. My dad was Ernest O. Lawrence. He died prematurely in his late fifties, only fifty-seven years old. It was a shock. I was only seventeen at the time. It was extremely hard.

I'm so sorry. What happened?

He had ulcerative colitis that was made worse by stress. He was sent to Geneva to represent the United States in disarmament talks with the Soviets and became very sick when he was there. The doctors had recommended years before that he have his colon removed. He was so sick that, when he returned home, he relented on having the surgery. He went to Stanford and died on the operating table.

After he died, both laboratories—the Lawrence Berkeley Laboratory and the Lawrence Livermore Laboratory—were named after him. They became national laboratories by an Act of Congress.

Did he start both labs?

Yes, and was the initial director of both. After his death my mother became an activist against nuclear proliferation and joined the anti-nuclear movement. Molly was on a campaign to get my father's name removed from the Livermore Lab—which was more of a weapons lab. The Berkeley Lab has mostly been pure research, not weapon oriented. She felt that the Livermore Lab was part of the problem of nuclear proliferation. She lobbied for this and she tried to get our congressman to help.[24] While she was alive, I never let her know how I felt about her actions.

My personal opinion is, if my dad were alive he would have been proud to be associated with both laboratories and that the work at Livermore served to lessen the chance of war. Rather than making the United States look evil, I believe he would have thought it put us on a more equal footing with the Soviets. I believe that is what happened. I thought it was really unfair for Molly to try to get his name removed from the Lab. The names were never changed, because it would have required another act of Congress to reverse it. No one was willing to push that through. Her wishes were never fulfilled.

My perception is that what my father did was honorable and useful and he would be proud. It is something my mother turned out not to be proud of. But that was her prerogative. I didn't agree with her.

After my father's death I reconnected with Lawrence Livermore Lab. I had not been there since I was a kid. When I was a child, my dad used to drive me there and I would wait at the guard shack while he was inside. I would go in the shack and play and visit with the guards. I went there with my wife on July 7, 2003, and they gave us a wonderful tour. We spent the whole day there. They pulled out the red carpet for us. There were photo ops everywhere, and they showed us all the different facilities. It was impressive.

A great deal of what they do is, of course, peace-time-oriented. They work on conservation, counterterrorism, energy, and laser projects. The laser project is interesting because it provides a means of testing nuclear weapons in a micro atmosphere so that you never have to do a nuclear test again. It can be done with a laser and computer instead of with a real bomb.

What did your father tell you about his work on the Manhattan Project?

When I was a kid, my father never talked about his work at home. He always said it was a military secret. He was extremely security-minded. I was only a toddler when the Manhattan Project was going on and wasn't capable of understanding until I was older what it was about. When I went with him to the Lab I enjoyed the collegial relationships that all the scientists had. They had great respect for one another. I met nuclear scientists from all over the world, and we would have parties. There were Soviets and sometimes Japanese. It was kind of fun for a kid to have parents like that.

Other than my mother, I was never aware of any thought in the family that there was concern or shame or regret that my father had done what he had done. I never felt any of that. I believe that the bomb actually saved lives in the long run. If the war had continued, there would have been many more Japanese and Americans who would have died before the war would have come to an end. I believe it was mostly a good thing. On the other hand, it started a nuclear-arms race and I'm not sure that was good; fortunately, now I think that threat is mostly over.

The concern we have now is the rogue nations like Iran that would like to have nuclear capabilities. Of course, some places like India have nuclear capabilities, and there is the problem of them getting in some kind of altercation with Pakistan. We are still dealing with the nuclear age, but nothing like back in the sixties. It's been a vast improvement.

I'm reading a book called A World Destroyed: Hiroshima and Its Legacies *by Marin J. Sherwin. It tells the story of Niels Bohr before he talked to Roosevelt and then Churchill and the bomb was completed. He looked into the future and realized there would be an arms race. Nobody took him seriously; they all thought he was kind of a crackpot. He thought Roosevelt took him seriously, but behind his back a deal had already been made for a postwar pact with Churchill.*

Roosevelt had?

Yes, to keep bombs and secrets inside the United States and Britain. Roosevelt found out that somebody gave the idea to the Soviets that this was going on and already knew, but Bohr wanted Roosevelt to tell Stalin to avert an arms race. Of course, it was not the only time the scientists' opinions were ignored by the government.

Somebody communicated with the Soviets and told them that the project was being done. Of course, at that time, the Soviets were our allies. It wasn't quite indecent but it probably wasn't supposed to be done.

I don't think Oppenheimer was ever disloyal; he might

have passed secrets to the Soviets, but I think it was someone else. I think he was falsely accused by the House Un-American Activities Committee. He was finally exonerated years later.

He had gone to a few Communist party meetings with his first wife and was not interested. They held that over him. There were very paranoid people in those days. I found a letter that my father wrote in support of a man who worked at the Joliet Ammunitions Plant in Illinois during the Joseph McCarthy Red Scare. They were investigating whether he could be trusted and was a patriotic citizen.

Probably the best book I've read about the era is *Tuxedo Park: A Wall Street Tycoon and the Secret Palace of Science That Changed the Course of World War II*, by Jennet Conant, who is James Conant's granddaughter. Alfred Lee Loomis was a wealthy philanthropist, a physics groupie, and a great friend of my family. He wasn't a trained physicist but he loved physics and physicists. He set up a private laboratory in his mansion back east in a place called Tuxedo Park in New York. Scientists would go there and stay for weeks at a time. My dad was there, and many other physicists spent time there collaborating and conducting research. The work they did there they could not do in their research or academic positions and it was entirely funded by Loomis, which was apart from the Manhattan Project.

Shortly before Dad died in the mid-1950s, we traveled to Europe. Soon after we returned, we were home and, at around ten o'clock at night, the phone rang. He didn't normally answer the phone but decided that, with somebody calling this late at night, it must be important. It was the Lab. While on the phone his face turned ashen. We became very concerned and wondered what happened. He hung up the phone and he said "I've got to go. It looks like the Soviets are trying to pull something. They may be attacking us."

What year was that?

It was around 1954 or '55. At the time they didn't know what had happened but assumed the Soviets had released a radiation cloud and were trying to destroy us. That's what he thought. He jumped in the car and went back to the Lab so they could measure and monitor the situation. He told us, "Stay indoors, close all the windows, fill all the bathtubs with water, and just sit tight and wait until you hear from me."

Why fill the bathtubs?

My dad said, "If the water is cut off or contaminated, at least you would have water for a while." It was really scary. When he returned home, we found out there was a thirty- or forty-fold increase in radiation everywhere that could be measured in Northern California. It turned out that it was from a Russian nuclear test that rose into the atmosphere. It was carried over by the jet stream and dumped on Northern California. The Soviets were not attacking; but, at the time, it was interpreted as an act of war.

If it was a cloud from a Russian nuclear test that had been blown by wind currents, would it have come all the way from Europe? Did it blow over the whole United States?

I'm not really sure what direction it came from. It was in the newspaper, so I think you can look up "radiation scare from Russia in the 50s." [*I could not find this, but it could have been deliberately kept out of the newspapers.*]

Did you have any scares other than that time?

I remember, many years ago, my dad was driving to work [and] he heard what sounded like a rock strike the car.

It turned out to be something stuck in his car door, but there was the fear that somebody might have tried to shoot him. When I was around nine or ten, we had a Secret Service agent living with us to protect my dad, and, probably more than anything else, to keep him from talking or saying something he shouldn't. He acted as a chauffeur.

Did you ever discuss your dad's work or the legacy of the Labs with your siblings?

We occasionally talked about Molly and her campaign to remove my dad's name from the Lab. I think one or two of my sisters were in favor of changing the name. The rest of us— there are six children—were in favor of leaving it the way it was. We didn't spend a lot of time discussing it. We didn't want to upset Molly.

Do you have any unique memories related to this unusual heritage we both share?

To me, it's all positive. I have no negative feelings, regrets, misgivings, or concerns. I think the end result of my dad's work has been far more positive than negative. We were going to enter into a new age one way or the other. It was just a matter of who was going to usher in the nuclear age. Many people were working on the same thing at the same time. My father started the ball rolling with the cyclotron. Had he not done that, someone else would have invented it. I think he did it in good conscience and with responsibility.

At first my father was very much against the use of any of these weapons. At some point the scientists wrote a letter to Truman telling him not to do it.

Right, my father signed the petition from the Met Lab.

Then again, dropping the bomb was probably the right

thing to do. It ended the war sooner and saved lives. Though there's no doubt that the effect was horrible, seeing the pictures of Hiroshima and Nagasaki.

What is far more awful is what's going on right now. I'm ashamed of the United States; I'm ashamed to be an American in a country where someone pisses us off and then we attack. It's ridiculous that there are three countries we are at war with; Iran, Afghanistan, and Iraq, under the guise of fighting terrorism. It's Saudi Arabia where Osama bin Laden was from, but we don't touch them, because we need their oil and they need us. The idea of America declaring war on other countries is unthinkable to me, yet it's happened two or three times in the past ten years. Congress has never approved it. I thought Congress had to approve a war! I guess not. Apparently the president can just get on the phone and say go ahead and attack.

Vietnam was never declared a war, not even Korea. World War II was the last declared war.

I don't know what's wrong with this country. What could possibly come of these wars? How could we possibly gain anything? There is no way we are going to change anything in the Middle East. We are not going to change the way Muslims think about us. There's nothing we can do to change that. The more wars we have, the more sentiment there is going to be against us.

I completely agree!

I think it's unconscionable what we're doing now— far worse than what we were doing back in the Manhattan Project era. We should be done with wars; they are not legitimate. There is no excuse for it.

Chapter 13

Wendy Wallin

Wendy contacted me through the Manhattan Project website. Her father, Wally Wallin, worked at the Met Lab at the University of Chicago and later as a civilian scientist at the China Lake naval base in Southern California, where Wendy lived as a child. When we spoke on the phone in 2013, Wendy had just finished writing a book about her family and their time at China Lake.

What prompted you to write your book?

My book focuses mainly on China Lake, where we moved when the war was over. My father was recruited to work for the Navy as a civilian scientist. I lived there from age two-and-a-half to nine. I am a marriage-and-family therapist and have worked short-term assignments with military members and their families.

A couple of years ago I was recruited for an assignment. This was a different kind of assignment than I had been doing with the military, a summer camp for children. The recruiter was surprised when I enthusiastically said I would take China Lake. It was one of the hardest to fill because it was summer in the middle of the desert. It was remote and far from what many would consider a pleasant place to live.

Going there made me want to examine my life when I was young. I wanted to know what my parents were like as young parents with their whole lives ahead of them. I was curious as to what my father felt as he transitioned from the Manhattan Project to working as a scientist with the military.

I have letters my parents wrote during those years. I had looked at them before but began examining them more deeply. I wanted to know how it was for them to physically relocate to a place that had hardships, although the Navy did their best to make the highly educated scientists comfortable.

In my book I focused somewhat on the Manhattan Project and my father's role. The idea of having been recruited for the Project set his path in life and his profession. For the rest of his life he worked on military projects where there were sites for either developing bombs or reconnaissance. I had a hard time teasing out what types of things he had done for the military. I'm sure my mother had a lot of mixed emotions about his work. The book is about their lives, their beliefs, who they were, and what was passed on to us despite my father working for the cause of destruction.

You must have a deeper view of that, being a therapist and having worked with people in the military as a therapist. How did you see your father's involvement in the Manhattan Project and later, the military, affecting you and your siblings?

There are different levels. The logistical levels affected my sister more profoundly, and that carried on throughout her life. Those influences were much less with my brother. He was only three years old when my father went to work at the Met Lab. The desert had negative effects on everybody except me, because I was only two-and-a-half and this was my life. I was a desert rat.

What intrigued me was what it was like for my mother. When my father began work in Milwaukee, we stayed behind for six months. He was looking for housing and was recruited for the Project. He worked a forty-hour-a-week job and also three days a week at the Met Lab in Chicago.

Wow! Do you know who recruited him?

George Monk was who my father ended up working for. It might have been that he asked to have him recruited. My father received a letter asking him if he might be interested in working on a special project. The letter may have been from someone working at the Met Lab.

For my sister, being a five-year-old who was daddy's little girl, it probably devastated her. Not being able to go to Milwaukee for six months must have been really hard for her.

I was never able to talk to my mother about how she felt after the bombs were dropped. I never knew how to. At my father's level they didn't let the spouses in on them being dropped until afterwards. He was a consultant three days a week. I'm sure he knew something, but not the big picture. I'm really not sure if he knew or wasn't supposed to talk about it.

How much each scientist knew depended on how high up he was and his or her "need to know." I don't think any of the scientists were allowed to speak about the dropping of the bombs before it happened. But a lot of their spouses figured it out, especially those at Los Alamos.

I suppose he told my mother after the bombs were dropped on Hiroshima and Nagasaki that that was the special project in Chicago. I could have asked my mother if I was a little more proactive.

When we were at China Lake we would go to my father's workplace, but he wouldn't talk about what he was working on; all we knew was that it was military work. The secrecy carried over after the war. The attitude was to make the best of a bad situation, to look at the positive side. We were trained in denial.

I was trained to look at the negative side of things, but that is just the other side of denial.

My parents were very optimistic, very progressive, liberal, and almost radical—except that they accepted the status quo on some levels. There was a dichotomy. There would be a rant from time to time, like a letter to an editor. It was done with the hope that we could make things better.

My parents were also liberal, always voted Democratic, and were against the Vietnam War. My dad was in a carpool from the early sixties and they always recycled.

They trained us in denial about the part we played in making things worse. His drinking and smoking were all part of that denial, and basically he drank and smoked himself into an early death at fifty-eight. But his attitude was all in fun: it doesn't hurt me, my doctor says it is better I drink than take Valium or other relaxants.

Does this really go back to his work on the bomb? I don't think in my book I said specifically; but yes, on some level for me it does. I don't know what to call it, but there's an awareness that there is this terrible thing in the world and, if we have contributed to it, all we can do is to do something to remedy it.

Oppenheimer said, "The physicists have known sin; and this is a knowledge which they cannot lose." [25] *I believe those ideas carried over to many people: the scientists, their families to some degree, and the rest of the world as well. For some reason, I took on the guilt and it propelled me to this project of my own. It is interesting that your parents went down the path of optimism; mine, pessimism and sarcasm. Part of that was being Jewish. It is traditionally reported how Jews have survived—making sarcastic jokes, making light of the dark.*

We had that too, but with an air of levity, an attitude of "We know better." Wally, my father, was sarcastic and cavalier as well. He didn't know how to deal with his involvement in the military and being a part of developing the bomb. I believe he was always trying to resolve it. At the same time there was the attitude that we can still do the right thing and make things better.

You mentioned that your father's military work may have had more of an effect on your sister than on you or your brother. Can you elaborate?

First, I don't know exactly when she knew about the Manhattan Project, but she was an adult then. She died at thirty-five of pulmonary hypertension secondary to a congenital heart defect. We never knew she had a heart issue before she died.

So sad; I am sorry.

Living in China Lake was difficult for her. She was a difficult child.

In what way?

Angry, acting out; she was sexually active at a very young age—twelve or thirteen. That seemed to happen more on a military base. My sister didn't want to have much to do with the family. In the book I partially psychoanalyzed her. She had a big effect on me because of her anger. I have asked myself what I can trace it back to. Was it my father leaving, competition with my brother, me being born at the time my father left for those six months? The fact that he was so caught up in his work and he wasn't available to her the way he had been with us? She was angry—emotionally abusive to me in a sense—and it contributed to a lot of my insecurities.

That sounds a bit like me and my sister, who is six years older, born in 1946 right after the war.

How do you think the legacy of the Manhattan Project and living on a military base has affected your life? You went into psychology.

My father being an alcoholic and my sister's influence affected me as an adult. I think that my father spent his life doing something he really didn't want to do, starting with his work at the Met Lab. However, he wrote to my mother in a letter, "I will think of these days at the University of Chicago as the happiest of my life." There was something seductive and addictive about the work with other scientists and being completely involved in a significant project. He wanted to contribute to the war effort and that was his way to do it. It sucked him in and he ended up working for the military the rest of his life. He probably didn't want to, but that was where the money was.

People respected him. At one point he became involved in Panavision and was one of the founding partners. He designed the PV lens that they used to make wide-screen movies. He thought that would be an out for him and did some more work for the movie industry, but then he sold his partnership. They didn't think they would have any more work for him since they already had the lens.

There were many opportunities in research. My father worked at Argonne National Lab after the war until he retired. The laboratory was government funded, and one of the spokes that led off the wheel of the cyclotron was bomb development. He loved his work, but his passion was— as I am sure with many others—pure scientific research. Unfortunately, the opportunities for that were slim, since funding was mainly for weapons development.

My father had the connections through Cal Tech from his work at China Lake, which helped him in his consulting business. My mother became his unofficial assistant.

After his work with Panavision he went back to the work he could do for the military. I do not know how the awareness of what he was working on affected him, but he did become more radical than he had been. He was antiwar but still involved in work related to nuclear bombs. I saw him in some ways as a discordant human being.

It reminds me of my cousin saying he believed my uncle, who had worked on the H-bomb, thought it kept the peace better than the A-bomb. No one would dare use the H-bomb, but the A-bomb had been used.

My father avoided himself by drinking and using sarcastic humor. He would sometimes write letters to the editor about what was wrong with the world.

My mother called China Lake a schoolboys' holiday where they had fun and flew airplanes. She thought it was time for him to actually make something of himself. My father felt like a cog in a large wheel there.

He was a cog in the military machine. Then you ended

up back at China Lake for your assignment as a therapist.

I think it is ironic that I was back in China Lake. After completely throwing out the military all my life I realized my life had been basically supported by the military. I had gone to school in China Lake, and my father earned money from the Defense Department for me to go to college. So here I am: "Hi, Daddy."

I know what you're saying: What are the karmic lessons, what am I supposed to be learning? I would like to just get on with my life. [We both laugh.] One of the problems is that I've been working full time for so long and then I put my book aside for long periods of time. Although it is much more than that, I didn't really want to think about my connection to the bomb. It is like lying down on Freud's couch and trying to analyze the effect of the bomb on my psyche with a globe of the world in the chair next to me.

Opening to your first chapter, I realized this is what I've been looking for. I liked your Chapter Zero. Since I worked at China Lake I've wanted to find out more about the Manhattan Project, the workers—what they thought and felt. For me it is a little like setting aside one layer of denial. I have come to acknowledge through my work, my research, and writing my book that we are always going to have a military. The question is how do we reconcile having peace with having a military?

Good question. I don't know if it is possible, since the role of the military is to attack and defend. Unfortunately, many times the United States is the aggressor. The bomb was developed to stop the evil of Hitler; once it was out there, the plan was to keep anyone else from using it.

The reason for the deterrence of the Cold War and

détente: was we know you can blow us up and you know we can blow you up, so it was supposed to keep everything in check.

It's interesting, because I didn't know until I was talking to my cousin that my uncle had also worked on the hydrogen bomb. That was a major surprise to me. His view was that we're going to have an even bigger, better bomb that will keep everybody in check because nobody wants to use the A-bomb, let alone the H-bomb. More destructive weapons will keep a better peace. It is more than ironic.

You said your brother asked you if you knew your dad had worked on the Manhattan Project.

My brother must have been in college at the time and in high school when he was involved in the antiwar and anti-nuclear movements. He was at the University of California Berkeley, which was politically very radical. He had a conversation with my mother and she said with pride that Wally—we always called him Wally—had worked on the Manhattan Project and helped end the war. As far as I know, that was the essence of the conversation. My mother said that she didn't know about his work until the bomb was dropped. I don't think my brother ever talked about it with my father. At some point there was a general discussion when we were sitting in the living room, and my brother said my father was involved in the Manhattan Project. I think, at the time, I had it confused with some positive event or social movement—like helping to end the Spanish Civil War or the Lincoln Brigade. It wasn't until much later, when I was in middle age, that I understood about the Manhattan Project. I then realized that was what Wally was working on. It never crossed my mind that he shouldn't be working for the military. That's the position

I took.

That's optimism, or optimistic denial, which sounds like an oxymoron.

My father didn't want to know too much and, therefore, was able to maintain a certain level of optimism. After transferring to another university, I returned to UC Berkeley. My father was able to get me a job while I was going to school at a place called Nuclear Research Instruments in Berkeley. It was near a spice factory near Ashby Avenue and San Pablo Street. Whenever you got off the freeway you could smell the spices. I never knew exactly what they were doing but believed they were building early computers for reconnaissance work. I recently tried to look it up on the Internet but couldn't find any information on it. The computers were in the back room. I was responsible for copying blueprints.

What year was that?

It was 1964, about the time I wrote my father's bio for the Optical Society of Southern California. I really began wondering what he had done on the Manhattan Project. He either contracted with them or they contracted with him in terms of him developing reconnaissance technology.

A lot of documents have been declassified. Some of them are on the Manhattan Project website. You said your dad was very secretive. Can you elaborate?

He didn't talk about it directly, but I believe he tried to pass the knowledge on to me indirectly through comments about one thing or another—comments, for example, about Edward Teller. I was in his physics class, by the way.

That must have been strange—somewhat ironic.

He was one of the few professors who I actually took

time to see. I went to the midterm exam—and when I walked in I realized it was like having a recurring dream where you haven't read the textbook. I sat down and realized I didn't know anything. I told Teller I had a really bad headache and couldn't take the exam, and he let me take a makeup exam.

Lying to Edward Teller—now there is an interesting concept. What was he like as a professor?

He just stood up there and lectured. I hardly remember. It was basic physics and very uninteresting. It wasn't like taking a class from Richard Feynman. That would have been much more interesting.

Definitely! Now there was a physicist who made it fun! He was probably the wittiest scientist who ever lived. My cousin Daniel Abraham said, "Everyone wanted to be Feynman." I can't imagine Teller was very happy with having to teach a basic physics course.

Edward Teller developing the hydrogen bomb only affected me indirectly. What I understood from my father was that atomic weapons are bad and we have to do something to mitigate their threat. His thinking was that we had this horrible weapon but we should never use it. He wrote a facetious comment about Teller. He said, "As a scientific worker, it is relatively easy to understand [Edward] Teller's point of view with respect to the proposed treaty with Russia. Two small bombs served to end World War II, and the most fascinating aspects of his work have not been effectively demonstrated. Only a third world war can provide him with the demonstration that his life's work has not been in vain."[26]

That's poignant!

When I was in college I went with my mother, father, and

a friend to see the movie "Dr. Strangelove," loosely based on Teller. I don't remember the discussion afterwards; he didn't say he had worked on the A-bomb—I just remember my father asking me what I thought of the movie. It left a strong impression on me, and I don't believe I conveyed that to him. I became more resolute in my understanding of nuclear weapons being negative.

And yet he continued to work for the military.

Was it denial? Was it rationalization? I'm not sure. Perhaps his thinking was, if I could make sure we know where the weapons are that play a role in preventing nuclear conflagration, then that will be my part.

It would have been fascinating to know what Teller would have said if you were in his office and said something about your dad working on the Project.

Yes, the eternal what if. That's another part, that it's not about the nuclear weapon; it's about the secrecy.

Right. That secrecy, I think, has undermined a lot of what could have been done and what could have been communicated.

I agree—between me and my dad, my mom, my sister.

Yes, I think it was a large part of my family and with other people I interviewed. Their experiences also came packaged in secrecy.

Once he had the security clearance lifted he could talk about anything. You never knew where the boundaries were.

Do you remember when he was granted clearance?

I'm not sure, when but the letter he wrote about security clearance was around the fall/winter of 1943, when he began work at the Met Lab. He may have also gone through another clearance process before working at China Lake.

What did your mother do?

She was mostly a housewife and mother. She had wanted to be a teacher but helped my father when he developed his business. She took some classes and learned about developing lenses. He always had an office not far from where we lived, and my mother became vice-president of his company. She did accounting and administrative work, but also ray tracing[27] to design lenses.

My brother became a lawyer, and his first career position was providing legal aid. I wanted to get as far away from the military as I could; but ironically, I was the only one who went to the military in any respects. I joined the Peace Corps soon after I graduated from college. My mother was a bit freaked out, but still proud. My father was proud of me and loved hearing the stories I wrote to him. I believe, for him, it was compensating in some way for his work. I was doing something for peace, on the other side of the equation of making bombs. I missed most of the antiwar movement when I went to Niger in West Africa—near Mali and Nigeria.

What kind of work were you doing there?

I was what they called a B.A. [Bachelor of Arts] generalist, someone just out of college who basically didn't know shit. My first assignment was called "Animation Feminine." The concept was to teach skills to women that would hopefully result in paid work so they would not be completely beholden to their husbands. I was later moved to a different town and worked as a health educator. I taught women nutrition and how to prevent early childhood death.

Chapter 14

Kristi Grove

Kristi was not yet born when her father labored up the hill at the University of California Berkeley campus in the middle of the night to the cyclotron to avoid taking a cab and arousing suspicion. When she responded to my email request for interviews, I learned that she lived in the San Francisco Bay Area, and I suggested we meet. She wrote back that she lived in the East Bay in a place I had "probably never heard of" called El Sobrante. I laughed, because it turned out we lived right down the street from each other.

Our first meeting was at the Borders bookstore in Emeryville. We visited briefly at the bookstore's café tables. She showed me her father's interview with Studs Terkel in his book The Good War: An Oral History of World War II, *and we began to get to know each other a bit before she had to run to an appointment. A few weeks later, we sat down for a more leisurely interview at my home, where we sipped mint tea as my cat studiously ignored us.*

My father, John Hite Grove, was a chemist at the University of California Berkeley during the war. I don't know exactly what his position was, but he had bachelor's degrees in chemistry and physics and was somehow recruited into the Project. They didn't tell him the Project was the atomic bomb. It only took him about a week to figure it out.

My dad lived in Albany, and they would call him in the middle of the night and say we need you right away. Sometimes he'd have no gas and he couldn't take a taxi because he was afraid people would notice and wonder why he was taking a taxi at that hour. He didn't know who was and wasn't a spy and thought it possible the driver could be one. He walked all the way from Albany up to the radiation lab, a six-mile uphill hike, just to avoid arousing suspicion.

That is pure dedication to his work and the secrecy of the Project.

One incident made him extremely angry. He told me he had to be very careful what he said on the phones, because he never knew whether they were tapped. One of the scientists had called and asked a lot of questions about what they were working on and my dad said to him: "We cannot talk on this phone. You don't know who is listening." He was very upset that he had put them both at risk.

How old were you when you knew he worked on the atom bomb?

The earliest I remember was in elementary school, but of course I didn't understand the whole scope back then. He liked to tell stories about the people he worked with at the Lab.

What do you remember?

He told me about this scientist who was a real practical joker who worked in the Lab. One scientist asked my dad if he could borrow his Bunsen burner. Then he hooked it up to the water line so when another scientist turned it on, water hit him in the face. He was really angry and didn't believe that my dad was not behind it.

Another story he told me was about a woman who always showed up to work in gorgeous silk dresses, even though those fabrics were really hard to get during the war because of clothing rationing. No one could get clothing like that without a connection.

Who did she know?

Exactly! Something happened, and chemicals were spilled on her skin and dress. They had to drag her down the hall and throw her into a safety shower because there weren't any in the Lab. She was fighting them the whole way because water and silk don't mix and she did not want her dress to be ruined. They dragged her into the safety shower anyway.

She would have rather had chemicals on her?

I know, he said that she always came to work in these gorgeous dresses. I said to my dad that maybe she was a spy or knew somebody in the black market.

He told me that, around the beginning of the war, some Americans didn't think the Japanese were a threat, because they didn't think they were very good pilots. He said he heard people say that they couldn't be very good pilots, because their eyes were so slanted—so how could they really see well enough to fly?

It's amazing that they would say that!

This was the way some Americans thought. There was rampant racism at the time, so they weren't really very worried about them as pilots. Of course that changed, because more and more Japanese pilots weren't afraid to die—the kamikazes.

Exactly. America, at that time, saw Germany as a

threat, not Japan.

My dad said that the day they dropped the bomb they heard it on the news like everybody else.

I didn't know if my father knew before they dropped it. I knew that they kept everything compartmentalized—certain people only knew a small part of the project, basically only what they were working on. Depending on how high up you were, that was how much of the picture you knew.

When he heard the announcement on the radio, he said, "Oh my God, oh my God, what have we done?" He was devastated; the difference between the creation of the Project and the reality of the destruction was overwhelming to him. One man he had been working alongside was jumping around and said, "We took those guys down," and made horrible racist comments. My father lost all respect for him after that; he didn't tolerate racism. He knew these were civilians; mothers and children, and not the military.

His brother, who was a fighter pilot during the war, told him years later that scientists saved our lives. "You demoralized them; that's why they quit. They surrendered, and you saved so many American lives." I don't think my father ever completely believed that. He believed in what he did because we didn't know how close Germany was. Nobody knew. They imagined that Germany was far ahead and the focus was on getting the bomb first. It was a race. Yet neither side really knew what the other side was doing, so the pressure was extreme.

My father was a delegate to the Atoms for Peace conference in Geneva and signed the petition to stop the bomb from being dropped. Do you know if your father ever took part in anything like that?

I don't think he protested that, but I know he joined a couple of Vietnam protest marches. I was very young at the time, five, and he didn't want to put me in the middle of that. There was a time when they thought there would be a riot, so instead of being part of the march he served Wyler's Lemonade and oranges to the marchers.

The most profound story my dad told me was one that affected the rest of his life. Something went wrong with what they were working on. It was during the war, it was an extremely serious situation. He never said exactly, but it was a meltdown or something. It happened up on the hill in Berkeley, and it had the potential to be far-reaching if they didn't stop it. The scientists got together and they drew straws; my dad and this other man lost. They were expected to go out into the field and manually shut everything down. The other guy freaked out and ran. My dad went out to the field and he manually shut down whatever it was. He was out there for five or six minutes. That was really the turning point in his health; he never recovered.

That is so tragic and sad.

Yes, it was tragic.

What kind of health issues did he have that he thought were related to that incident?

In the beginning, he didn't have much of an immune system; if anyone would have a cold he would catch it. For the longest time there weren't any horrible long-term effects.

There was no protective clothing?

There wasn't time. It had to be done right then; there was no time to suit up. They probably had some straws sitting around, drew them, and that was that. He went out there alone and did what he knew he had to do.

At first the effects were not great, not like with the people at Chernobyl. By the time I was three or four years old, he started becoming very ill and losing sensation in his hands and feet. He'd go to doctors and they thought he was a hypochondriac. But he knew something was wrong. One time he passed out in the hospital. They were able to bring the circulation back, but he lost the motor nerve to one foot. He suffered from two different diseases, Herpes Simplex Zoster [which they knew very little about at the time] and polyarteritis nodosa (PAN). The diseases attacked his circulatory system and most likely other parts of his body. He had to take medication—I can't remember the name of it, but it's a steroid. They don't like to give it to people for a very long time, and it makes you gain a lot of weight.

Prednisone?

Yes, that's it. All the medications he took were hard on his body. He didn't sleep well; he also suffered from chronic pain and [that] caused difficulty sleeping. Somehow, though, they were able to get him back into remission. I remember when I realized how serious it was. We had gone to a movie— interestingly enough it was about World War II. It was an English movie and it was about a boy's experience from a ten-year-old's point of view, I don't remember the name. All of a sudden my father gasped, and I shook him and cried, "Dad, Dad," and I'm thinking he's dead. The first thing I had to do was to look in his pockets, get his keys, and get someone who could drive. My mind was racing. I dropped my popcorn, and then he said, "Why did you drop your popcorn?" He came to, but he had passed out and, at the time, I didn't realize how serious it was. I just said, "Dad!" I really should have rushed him to the hospital, but I just didn't know what to do. *How would you know? You were just eleven.* When I was about twenty-three, he came out of remission and his blood platelets started dying. His blood platelets were very low, but they were able to get him back into remission. When he came out of remission this time, his white blood cells decided his red blood cells were enemy antigens and they were attacking them. He became horribly anemic, and it was extremely serious. Once a week he had to go to the hospital to receive immunoglobulin. He was in the hospital several times. I was at college at the University of California Davis when he started to get worse. He had always looked young for his age, but he aged rapidly. In a short time, he went from looking like he was in his sixties to his eighties. He developed a weird skin condition because he had reactions from two of the medications. The doctors couldn't figure out which ones, so he did his own research from his home library and some books he had me check out from the public library. He figured it out, because the doctors weren't able to.

That year he died. After he went into the hospital, I got a call from mom, and I said, "Oh, should I come back?" She said she thought he wasn't going to make it the previous night, but that he seemed fine. I went back to school and then, two days later, I got a phone call at four o'clock in the morning, and he'd had a massive heart attack. When I arrived, the doctor was beside herself because she really liked my dad and she felt guilty that she didn't save him. I remember her crying. I'm holding the doctor and said, "It's okay. I know you did what you could."

You were comforting the doctor?

I know. I was thinking, there is something really weird about this picture, but I didn't want her to experience guilt. She was young, and I knew she did everything she could. After he died they found that he was in the beginning stages of liver cancer, so we were kind of glad that he died before that took hold. He was always afraid of cancer; he was spared that at least. He went fast.

In a way—twenty years or so.

Well, yes. He was only supposed to live five years with his disease, which is why my parents didn't have any more children. He lived more than twenty years, though. My mother thought she could not handle having more than one and probably thought, if he died, she couldn't raise two children alone.

Did he ever get compensation?

No. This was his belief: there were many people sacrificing themselves during the war by going into the military. They performed very noble acts—going to war, fighting on foreign soil, and protecting our country. He felt that this was the war that he fought, and he did it for our country. He was very patriotic and believed in the stars and stripes. He said, "I lost my life in a certain sense and I did it for the greater good, so why should I look for compensation?" A lot of friends asked why he didn't sue. My dad felt you do not sue for protecting your country.

One of my friends had asked me how my father got a radiation disease, and it was really hard to talk about that as well.

After the war everybody was so scared about communism and the Joseph McCarthy Red Scare. My poor dad: his first wife was a bohemian woman and was interested in communism and the Communist party—it was the "in" thing with artists. She kept pestering my father to go to a meeting, so he finally went and he thought it was stupid. Because his wife was associated with the group, and he had been to a meeting, I often wondered if that could have been why he had difficulty finding work. He may have signed a roster or petition. He told me they had the FBI watching our house and tapping our phones.

Before my dad married my mother, who was quite a bit different from his first wife, he told her, "The FBI is watching me. Are you going to be okay with marrying me?" My mom didn't care, but I don't know when they stopped surveillance on him.

Somewhat like the well-known story of Oppenheimer. He also went to a Communist party meeting with his first wife, also in Berkeley, and was hounded at the McCarthy hearings. He lost his security clearance, and that caused him dozens of problems. It basically destroyed him in many ways, personally and professionally. Many think it broke his spirit. Many of the people I talked to said their parents were watched by the FBI. One, Glen's father, had FBI surveillance up to the sixties.

It doesn't surprise me. My dad was always very bitter about the McCarthy Era and how some actors testified against some of their fellow actors. I thought, my God, Dad, just leave it alone.

He eventually went back to work at UC Berkeley, studying why Strawberry Creek [the creek running through the campus] was polluted.

Did the radiation from the lab up the hill, where he

*had worked for so many years, have anything to do with the
pollution?*

No, I don't believe they ever found that. They did find
one reason was that stray dogs' waste was running into the
creek from sprinklers. My father worked on that project for
the rest of his career. He was having heart problems and other
medical problems, so he retired at the age of fifty-four. I think
they were worried that, if he was going to have a heart attack,
there might be some kind of lawsuit. I don't really know. They
forced him into early retirement. He didn't have much of a
pension plan from Shell, so if he hadn't married my mom, he
would have had to live on social security and $238 a month.

*What do you think about your father's involvement in
the Project?*

I can understand why he got involved in it, [but] I think
the way they dropped the bomb on a civilian population and
not a military installation was wrong. I can understand why
he worked on it. It could have so easily been Germany that
developed the bomb first. Can you imagine the consequences?
My father, being my father, would have wanted to do something to end the war.

*Do you think that having a parent who worked on the
bomb affected you in any profound ways? I felt that I was
brought up within a different reality that only my family shared and that this had a major effect on how I looked
at things. I felt really separate from my surroundings. I
remember saying to a friend I had grown up with something about my dad working on the bomb. She was really
surprised that I had never mentioned it before. I felt like I
shouldn't have said anything, as if the secret was still in
some way a family secret.*

I don't see my father as being very secretive about it. He obviously didn't tell everyone in the world, but I did get the sense that it was not to be talked about with many people. I think that it affected me in a different way, because he was so bitter about the McCarthy Era; I never quite understood where that came from until after he died. I always wondered why he couldn't just let it go, not realizing how it had destroyed him so much. He gave up so much for this country, and to be treated like a criminal hurt him very deeply. For someone who was as patriotic as my father, who loved this country as much as he did, it was devastating. He sacrificed his health and the life he loved for this country—to help create this bomb, to save this country—and then to be treated like a criminal and a spy. To give secrets away to Russia would never have been considered by my father. He could no longer participate in the activities he loved: hiking, dancing, backpacking, skiing, and all the outdoor activities that he couldn't do anymore because of the weight that he gained due to the prednisone. I think the fact that they thought he was going to give away secrets destroyed him inside. I believe it created such a deep wound; that's why he never talked about that aspect of it.

That is so sad. Emotional scars on your soul can be much deeper than physical scars.

I think, in some ways, he compensated by being so incredibly moral about things and being very judgmental about anybody who he thought didn't live up to a certain moral code. Maybe because his moral code was not believed by our government, that made him hypersensitive. He was extremely judgmental about people, with high standards that most people couldn't live up to.

*I have found that so much in people that I have inter-
viewed; it's a theme that runs through most of us as a group.*

That moral streak made life very difficult; most of my
friends didn't live up to it, and certainly not the guys I went
out with. A high moral fiber predominated; and, if you stepped
out of line, it wasn't good. The other important aspect was
the ability to think and perform in school; mental capabilities
were the most important thing—your moral fiber and your
ability to use your mind. He didn't have any friends. He was
very ill and had to quit work when I was six. He became a
househusband—a Mr. Mom—when men were not doing that.

He stayed home and took care of me. My mom was the
one who worked. He did all the shopping and cooking. He
didn't houseclean; my mom ended up having to do that. It
was hard on him, because, back then, men were in charge
of the money in the household. My mother was making all
the money, but he had control over it, which was really very
weird to me. He would give her an allowance of sixty dollars
a month for clothes and other things. They both had grown
up very poor. Mom allowed him to take care of the money
because she knew that not doing so would be really hard on
him.

*Maybe she was giving him some of the sense of control
that he'd lost?*

I think it was more that my dad needed to be needed,
and my mother needed to have that father figure. He was a
father figure to her until she got older; she was very young
when they married. They were not intellectually compatible
at all.

My mother is extremely bright, but when my dad

was talking about his work I think she kind of tuned out, although she was very proud of him.

When my father became ill their marriage became based predominantly on emotional needs.

I think that was fairly common, especially in the fifties. It seemed it was intensified with your parents.

In the beginning it was based on an enjoyment of going hiking; they would hike forty miles into base camp. He took her ice camping, and they met folk dancing. When my father became ill he couldn't do a lot of those things. My father was at home and didn't have the intellectual outlet of going to work, and both my brother and I were turned into intellectual companions. My mother was cut out of a lot of things; at dinner conversation she couldn't keep up.

Do you think that his career is one of the reasons you went into chemistry?

I don't really think that's the reason. I actually wasn't planning to go into science until I was about twenty-three. I didn't do well in science and I didn't like math, but I think it was the curiosity that my dad fostered that made me go into science. It probably influenced me.

I barely got through my bachelor's degree. It was a real struggle; I had a really hard time and I was not a very logical, analytical person. I probably used about 90% of the other side of the brain, the most that you could possibly be—is it the right or the left side?

It's the right side, the creative and more intuitive side. Strangely, it also controls the left side of the body.

For me to develop the left, analytical side was really difficult. I would say I'm more 60/40 now. But at the time it was

85 to 90 percent creative and 10 percent scientific.

I relate to that because I started out as an art major in college. I'm a published poet and a photographer; creative pursuits were the way I seem to still use my mind best. I was scared to death to take a chemistry course, fearing not doing well or not understanding it. I didn't even really seriously start developing that part of my brain until I worked on a sleep-research project. I worked there for ten years and learned to analyze sleep data and to look at minute waveforms and interpret them. I really developed that part of the brain that deals with concrete details. I was completely going in the other direction, as well. I didn't want to have anything to do with science.

That's how I felt, too.

Part of me felt like, look where the science went, look what it created. I was afraid to be a part of anything that might even remotely have the potential for doing something like that. That was why the anti-science, anti-technology backlash of the sixties and seventies fit my mindset at that time.

I didn't really feel that so much, but one time when they brought some radioactive samples to this lab I was working in, I said, "You bring this in, [and] I'm not working on these samples." That's when that whole side of my father really came up. I told my boss, "I will not work on radioactivity; I want nothing to do with it. I don't care how safe it is, I see what happened to my father, and I'm not going to get what he got. I'm not going to have that happen to me."

What were they going to use it for?

I have no idea; they were just going to bring in samples

and analyze [them].

Was this where you are working now?

No, it was an environmental lab. They were talking about branching out and getting more work for the lab and were throwing out suggestions about what we could bring in. I didn't care if I was offered a lot of money to work with radioactivity. I know there are more safety precautions these days, but that's still where I draw the line.

What are your thoughts about Livermore Lab getting the contract to redevelop and improve on the old nuclear weapons?

I think that is extremely dangerous. We tell other countries like Iran, you can't have any kind of nuclear program. Iran is surrounded by Iraq and Afghanistan, so theoretically I can understand why they would be nervous and want to build nuclear weapons. From a security stance I don't want that to happen. I find it hypocritical that the United States says we are the only one who can maintain a nuclear program. There has to be one rule for everybody. I really think we are going in the wrong direction. It's a Pandora's Box. I believe we must protect our country, but not by building nuclear weapons.

There was a movie I saw when I was a child that always scared me. It took place in a small New England town. It is a picnic-like atmosphere where the entire town gathers. Then the lottery begins and the person who "wins" is the one who gets stoned to death—a ritual sacrifice. [This was based on the title story of Shirley Jackson's short-story collection, The Lottery.]

This story sounds familiar. When you said that I kind of gasped.

They handed stones to the three-year-old child of the main character so she could throw them at her mother. I was twelve years old when I saw this and I don't know what happened. I think my father came out of remission at the time and I remember freaking out and, for six weeks, not being able to sleep—I slept on the air mattress in my parents' bedroom because I was afraid to be alone.

Periodically throughout my life I have been terrified of dying. I wouldn't be able to sleep, have horrible insomnia, and have to keep all the lights on. When I was older and began dating I would have to pass through a fear of death that sometimes would last a week or as long as a month. It would eventually subside and I could date that person without the fear of dying.

I wonder if the fear was related to the fear of your dad dying. He was so frail when you were a teenager and started dating.

I'm not sure; it was strange. I remember what would come to me was a quote from Shakespeare, and I would say it over and over in my head: "Cowards die many times before their deaths; the valiant never taste of death but once. Of all the wonders that I yet have heard, it seems to me most strange that men should fear; seeing that death, a necessary end, will come when it will come." [Julius Caesar 2.2]

If I repeated that enough I would be less scared. I have no idea why that quote would do that for me. It affected my whole life. There was nobody dying in other families I knew. Of course, I would never have talked to them about it because I thought they'd think I was weird or crazy. I remember during that time period when my dad was in remission, this woman who was the conductor of my orchestra committed suicide.

I went to the memorial service and I couldn't stop crying; I was hysterical and sobbing uncontrollably for several hours. It was very humiliating. I couldn't get control of myself.

How old were you then?

I was thirteen or fourteen. It was not specifically about her but, rather, about death. When my friend became very ill, her daughters were very concerned that she would not wake up. She thought it would be better if she didn't say anything to her kids. I said to her, "I guarantee they are coming up with something way worse than it is;" and she said she wanted to shelter them. I told her, "Don't shelter them; tell them what's going on." She had a long talk with them and she realized they had really crazy fears going on. I was helpful to her because I'd been through something so similar. I knew what it was like to have a parent very ill and, from a child's point of view, how terrifying it is. Kids know a lot more than adults realize.

Oh, of course, definitely! I can see why the movie The Lottery *had such a profound effect on you. It was your father in the lottery that day on the Berkeley hill; he drew the wrong straw that led him to lose his health and the life he had known. Who gets stoned in the town square and who has to go out and turn off the pipes? Who wins and who loses, whose life is changed forever?*

Yes, I think that was what it was. I never made the correlation before. It was probably that simple.

"Water and Silk Don't Mix," a poem written by the author inspired by my interview with Kristi, is at the end of this book in the section entitled Interview-Inspired Poems.

Chapter 15

Carol Caruthers

≋

Carol contacted me in the fall of 2006 after her daughter saw my ad on the Manhattan Project Heritage website. She spent time at Oak Ridge as a young child and was excited to talk with me about her father, who was an engineer there. As we talked on the phone, she told me of her home just outside Austin, Texas, with the Hill Country stretching out around her land and the Indian arrowheads that are still abundant just beneath the soil. I began by asking her what her first memory of Oak Ridge was.

≋

One day in 1942 some people came to our door in Chattanooga, Tennessee, and told my father, Stanley Blazyk, that he had to come with them. My mother asked, "Will you be home for dinner?" He said, "No. I can't tell you where I am going." My mother told me that the men told her they would get someone to tell the landlord we were moving. Soon afterward we were living in the secret city of Oak Ridge, Tennessee, in small, square, temporary housing on stilts they called *hutments*. No grass, just dirt all around.

My father went to college when he was sixteen years old. I don't know what specifically he did as an engineer at Oak Ridge. After the war he had his own engineering company.[28]

What do you remember about living in Oak Ridge?

We moved there just before my second birthday and lived there until the end of the war, when I was about four. My brother was born there. I learned to walk when I was nine months old and remember riding my bike around the town when I was older.

One incident that really had an impact on me was my father telling me to never play in the clay pipes that were around the area, that they were extremely dangerous. My friend Jimmy crawled into one and he became very scared. He was claustrophobic but was still afraid to come out. Even though I was so small myself I grabbed his leg and pulled him out. I was scared because of what my dad had told me. I told him and everyone else not to play in the pipes. Jimmy never went into the pipes again.

It turns out the radiation in the pipes was extremely high and just below ground level. My father knew all this and told us not to dig in the ground either.

That's pretty scary.

We lived there, but my mother and I didn't know what was going on around us. I have pictures I will send you of the houses. When we were in Oak Ridge my father planted two sycamore trees. Around 1980 my husband and I took our children to Tennessee and we went to Oak Ridge. I found the trees that were right where we had lived for those years. It was really exciting to see they were still there. We took our children to the museum that explained a lot of the history of Oak Ridge.

When I was in sixth grade in the fifties, we were living in Texas. The Korean War was going on and duck-and-cover

Carol as a child on the wooden sidewalks at Oak Ridge, Tennessee during the Manhattan Project.

drills were common, especially in the schools.

I remember them very clearly.

There was the big scare of the Soviet Union and an all-out nuclear war. The teacher picked me to be in charge of getting eight of the students to the correct place. I told her with great confidence, "Getting under the stairwell won't protect us from a nuclear bomb." She told me to be quiet, that I was scaring everyone half to death. They gave me a certificate for helping, but when I told my dad what I had said, he told me, "Just keep quiet and don't say anything more about it to anyone."

When we lived in Austin, Texas, there was a place on the south side of town that we used to always drive by. It sold tornado and bomb shelters. It was a huge outdoor store and warehouse that stretched along an entire block. The company was only there a couple of years. They started selling the shelters sometime in the fifties when there was the big scare of a war with the Soviet Union and the buildup of nuclear weapons. One year my father asked me what I wanted for Christmas. I told him all I wanted for my birthday and Christmas combined was a bomb shelter. He said, "You can't have one." I said, "I just want a little one." He said, "No." I decided that I would just go into one of the caves near where we lived if a bomb was dropped.

After I didn't get my own shelter, I memorized all the buildings in town that had the round, yellow-and-black signs that indicated a fallout shelter. I knew where every single one was. If a nuclear bomb was dropped, I was going to run into the closest one.

Good planning. I wasn't aware of any public shelters in the suburb I grew up in near Chicago, although someone built one in his backyard. I walked past it every day on my way to high school and thought about how strange it was and why he even bothered.

When I was thirteen I asked my dad, "Do you think the communists are going to get a bomb?" That would have been in 1955. He told me that it was harder than they thought to build one. Then he said, "I can't tell you any more than that." That was the end of the conversation.[29]

I used to go to the library on Saturdays and look up books that had information and pictures about the bomb. I think I was more curious than afraid, although looking at the pictures really did scare me. Years later, when I saw pictures of the aftereffects of hurricanes, with all the houses destroyed, the devastation reminded of the pictures that I saw in the library.

We had many tornadoes in the Midwest; towns would be just wiped out. I don't remember equating that with the bomb—but, then, you were closer to it, having actually lived in Oak Ridge.

Another thing that I clearly remember was the large chest-x-ray trucks that were driven around town. My father would not get within three-hundred feet of them and told us that radiation was all around the truck. He told my brothers and me that the people did not know the dangers they were taking getting x-rays. The radiation was so much more powerful back then; the rads were at much higher levels than they are now. They didn't even use the lead aprons they use today in dentists' offices. I thought about that when I worked in a dentist's office years later. I wanted to go in the truck to see what was inside, but my father told us we couldn't and were to never go inside one.

We moved to the country in 1954 and lived on a ranch my father bought outside of Austin. My mother was busy with the farm, and we were busy chasing goats and taking care of the cows. The Air Force jets from Bergstrom and San Antonio would occasionally fly overhead. The sonic booms and loud noises from the jets would sometimes bother my father. I always thought it was due to the sounds reminding him of the testing during the war, but I don't know. They always scared the poor chickens too. [Ruby Nelson mentioned the same reaction of her family's chickens in Chapter 11.]

My father's sister said that my father was always slightly introverted but became more so after the war. He became very quiet. He loved children so much, and I think he must have seen pictures of the children after Hiroshima, and it hurt him deeply. I think he just didn't want to talk about any of that, and that his work on the Manhattan Project contributed to his already quiet nature.

Are there incidents you can recall when you were older?

One incident that really shook me up was when I was in college. The FBI came to my dorm. My dorm mother came upstairs to my room and was very upset and confused. She said, "The FBI was just here. They asked whether you were enrolled here, what kind of car you have, and what your license number is. What did you do, anyway?"

I can see this panicked woman running up to your room, probably wondering who she had living under her roof!

I told my dorm mother, "Oh, it's probably something to do with my dad and his work." It unnerved me, though. I believe they followed a lot of the older children around during that time.

I can't imagine knowing the FBI was checking on you for the work your father did twenty years before. Especially since it was work that won the war.

Anything else you can would like to add?

I feel as if something scary will occur very soon.

Do you mean with all the wars in the Middle East?

I don't know, just something.

I hope you are wrong.

I do, too. Although these incidents have had a profound effect on my life, I believe it is important to remember the past, but not continue to live in it.

Chapter 16

Eric Holland

It is a slightly overcast November day in the San Francisco Bay Area; red and gold leaves frame the library where Eric Holland works. A mutual friend informed me that Eric's father was in Los Alamos during the war. She got us in touch, and we settled into a comfortable conversation in one of the private rooms in the Albany Public Library after Eric completed his work.

My father was Tom Holland. He worked at Los Alamos as a mathematician and physicist on the Nagasaki bomb. He had just finished his master's degree and was starting on his Ph.D. when he was drafted. He was in Patton's 75th Division and he received a secret communication that came from the company commander, who was not even aware of what the orders were inside. The commander was not happy about that. Next thing my dad knew he was shipped to Los Alamos. He didn't have a choice; he was a soldier.

The father of someone else I talked to had the same thing happen. It wasn't like with my dad, who was at the University of Chicago getting his degree in chemistry and recruited there for the Met Lab.

It was a good thing for my dad, because I understand

that Patton's 75th Division got hit really hard by the Germans at the Battle of the Bulge. Several of the guys he knew in basic training were killed.

Where was he getting his degree when he was drafted?

He was at the University of Rochester in upstate New York. He was a Southerner—grew up in Birmingham and went to college there. Then he went up to New York. He did not want to be drafted; maybe he was not so patriotic or just scared. I don't know.

Which group did he work with at Los Alamos?

His immediate boss was George Kistiakowsky,[30] and he worked on the timing of the Nagasaki bomb. He said he'd approach Richard Feynman when he had calculation problems. Feynman, who was his age, was someone he felt he could talk to, because everyone else was older. Feynman would walk around for about ten minutes and then give him the answer.

A very nice resource. How long was your dad at Los Alamos?

He was there for two years. He was drafted in 1943 and, ironically, after the second bomb was dropped, he developed an ulcer and received a medical discharge from the Army in September 1945. He didn't get the GI Bill because of that. The lab at Los Alamos recruited him immediately, but he was working on other projects.

Were his ulcers due to stress from working on the bomb?

He had ulcers before, but it definitely made them worse.

And he stayed in Los Alamos?

Yes, until 1954.

How many siblings do you have?

I had three. I have one remaining—my other two brothers are gone, but that's nothing to do with nuclear issues. I was born in 1948. [Almost an afterthought:] Enrico Fermi was my next door neighbor in Los Alamos. I was born there in 1948 and lived there until 1954 when I was five.

On your birth certificate, since you were born after the war, does it say P.O. Box 1663?[31]

No, but I had the same problem that Barack Obama had. It was a notification of birth—not an official birth certificate, which I was just recently able to get. Technically it's not a birth certificate. It's something else; and that's the problem that Obama had. It was so much bureaucracy, total B.S.

What do you remember about your time there?

I was just a kid and played outdoors a lot. I don't remember much but I do remember my parents telling me that we lived next door to Fermi and his wife Laura. We were watching something on TV and there was a picture of Fermi and his wife. My mom was laughing and said she used to babysit me.[32]

Did your dad ever talk to you about his time at Los Alamos?

He did a little. He told me he had to deal with Teller a lot and said that, in those days, Teller was a very sociable person. He told me his main memory of him was that he was the most intense person he had ever met. He didn't mention anyone other than Feynman and Teller.

Did you go to kindergarten there?

I just missed the cutoff for that.

Was there a fence around Los Alamos and were the labs still partitioned behind the fences at that time?

Yes, it was very barracks-like in some ways.

Were you in the Sundt Apartments? [33]

No, we were in a house. One time in high school we went across the country and drove into Los Alamos. It was kind of up from where the highway was and my dad pointed to a place and said we used to live there.

Were some of the scientists who were there during the war still there when you lived there?

Yes. There were other projects my dad worked on that weren't connected to nuclear weapons. Those were in the area of astrophysics, and my dad actually made a contribution in 1965. There was a man named Albert Michaelson, who won the Nobel Prize for Physics in 1907, who was an astronomer and a contemporary of Einstein. Michaelson figured out how to use light beams at different angles to measure distances in the universe and the diameter of stars—interferometry. He had different formulas for it, and even Einstein used it as a reference for relativity. My dad was looking at the calculations that had been time honored and found a mistake in the calculations. He was at MIT for some meetings and mentioned it to someone; I don't know who it was. He looked at it and realized my dad was right. He didn't get much credit for it. What I remember was that there was an article in our local paper.

It was a shame that he did not get acknowledged for such an important contribution.

We moved back to the East Coast in 1954, near where my grandparents lived. My mother wanted to go, but it was not my father's choice; he was working on things that he was interested in, which evolved into the field of astrophysics.

When they were back East he worked at Fort Detrick, it was then Camp Detrick, on the biological-warfare program—the U.S. Army Medical Command in Federick, MD, center of the biological weapons program from 1943 to 1969. He was the one who delivered the physics point of view that biological weapons were not deliverable. He said that it was not worth the trouble. That was his calculated opinion and it became the opinion that would become part of the Pentagon's official policy.

When was that?

Around 1960.

Changing focus, did you enjoy science?

No, I wasn't very good at that. My brother liked it and he became a meteorologist. I was like my mom; we are both interested in social-science history. I was good at that but not science or math. I hated math.

How many siblings do you have?

I have one brother and one sister, who lives in Stockton. She works as a nurse in the ICU. Thank God she's doing it because her husband's a building contractor. Since 2008 he hasn't worked a lot.

Did your father talk to you about his feelings working on the Manhattan Project?

My father was very antiwar and was strongly opposed to the Vietnam War—and to war in general. Of course, during Vietnam he had two sons who might have been drafted. He was worried about war, even before Vietnam, so his work on the bomb project must have had a negative influence on him. He was very distrustful of the government. He was the first person I knew who, from the beginning of the Vietnam War, did not want us to go.

I remember during the Joe McCarthy era there were at least a dozen people who were believed to have spied for the Russians. I remember as a kid of six seeing the pictures of them in 1954. [They included Morris Cohen, Klaus Fuchs, Harry Gold, David Greenglass, Theodore Hall, George Koval, Irving Lerner, Alan Nunn May, Ethel and Julius Rosenberg, Saville Sax, and Morton Sobell.]

There was a Russian general, Georgy Zhukov, who was the most decorated general officer in the Soviet Union during WWII. He was on the cover of Newsweek. I looked at the cover and I was impressed with his hat and medals; and I said, "Wow, I like that." And my mother said to me, "Don't ever say that outside this house." She was afraid because McCarthy was going after people in the government.

Because you were admiring a Russian?

Yes, a communist.

A lot of the scientists were followed for years, some decades, and everyone was checked out by the FBI.

I remember my dad saying he was giving a seminar or something, and some strange man would walk up to him and ask questions. He knew spying was going on and he wasn't comfortable at all with it.

How do you feel about the end of the war?

We won World War II; we were the only ones who did. When the war was over, half of the economic activity in the world went on in the United States. That was because all the industrialized nations from China to Europe committed suicide, so we had no competition—and people wonder why we can't go back to the fifties because everything was so great.

We were the economic engine, but that wasn't going to last forever.

Right. How do you feel about having a parent who worked on the Project? Did that affect you in any specific ways?

Mainly being aware of the Project and how the government might work—those are the main ways. One of my closest friends since childhood is Japanese-American, and his mother was in Hiroshima when the bomb was dropped. She died about thirty years ago of cancer. Ironically, my father and my friend's father were fairly close; so my dad knew what happened to her, and my friend knows all about what my father did during the war. My dad felt bad knowing that his friend's wife had died so young and probably due to radiation exposure.

My friend's father was the official censor for Sugamo Prison, where they tried and imprisoned Hideki Tojo for war crimes. He was basically the one censoring their mail. He had come to America before the war and went back to Japan during the war as a GI and ended up being a prison censor. It was hard to talk to him about it because he didn't say much of anything—a very quiet, but nice, man. It's too bad because I would have liked to have known more.

That's very interesting.

The Iraq War upset him more physically then I thought at the time. I would visit occasionally, and my sister called and said he had a heart attack and died. It was probably coincidental, but I don't know.

What was he specifically upset about?

He didn't like the United States being involved in military

interventions. From the beginning he was against Vietnam. I have wondered, if he were alive today, how he would have reacted to all that has happened in Iraq. I was glad my mom was gone by the time 9/11 happened. She missed that by a couple of months.

When 9/11 happened, my mother had an airplane ticket from California to Chicago the next day. She figured she could fly on the 13th. I said to her, "I don't think that you are going anywhere for a while." I don't know if it was because she'd seen so much in her life, but she said later on—when they had all the Homeland Security terrorist-alert warnings with the red, orange, and yellow levels—"They are just trying to make us afraid." She was right.

Are there other stories in relation to the bomb that your father shared with you in your childhood?

My father didn't really talk about it much. He did say, "We didn't know that much about radiation back then and didn't take a lot of safety precautions and should have."

Did he join the American Federation of Scientists or have any political affiliations related to that?

No, he wasn't much of a joiner. He voted for McGovern, and my mom was a conservative. They never discussed politics. I'll give her credit; she voted for Jimmy Carter over Ronald Reagan. She voted for George W. Bush because she didn't like Clinton because he had his pants down. [We both laugh.]

How do you see the state of nuclear weapons and nuclear energy today?

Fukushima! Chernobyl! Japan developed nuclear energy because they felt they had to. All their sources of energy came from imports; they had no oil and it wasn't cheap. They had to figure out how they were going to get their energy needs met.

True and extremely tragic and ironic that Japan, which banned making nuclear weapons after the war, would have such a horrendous nuclear accident.

We had a scientist in our neighborhood once who was my friend's father—Herbert Kroemer, who had won the Nobel Prize for Physics in 2000. I remember once I was sitting out on the hood of his car with his son and he made us get off. He said he didn't care about the car but there was something toxic, I guess in the paint. He was afraid it was going to get on our pants.

All those guys had pride in having beat-up old cars. We drove a '54 Ford for fifteen years. You'd think people like that wouldn't be that way, but people would talk about cars and my dad would say, "Yeah, when they go sideways let me know." They were not impressed with modern technology. [We both laugh.]

Only with nuclear physics, astrophysics, and cyclotrons—otherwise they were more interested in the non-material things that could only be studied by science. David Seaborg described it to me as the "spiritual aspect of science." [See Chapter 18.]

How was it moving back East after being at Los Alamos?

It was a farming community so, when you're a kid, you adapt. All my friends' fathers were dairy farmers. When I was in school, my friends' fathers were a bacteriologist and a dairy farmer, and that seemed completely normal. It's funny when I think back.

*Did you ever talk about your dad's work with your sib-
lings or with any friends?*

I told a few people, but not many, and I didn't really talk
about it with my siblings. Maybe because it wasn't his choice,
I didn't feel like there was some moral issue involved. My dad
was drafted into the Army and then transferred by orders into
the Manhattan Project. It was what he had to do and I thought
it was great that he didn't die in France.

The author, age five.

The author with her sister, Sheri, and brother, David, 1954.

Ellis P. Steinberg, the author's father, age 25, 1945. (courtesy of Argonne National Laboratory).

Bernard M. Abraham, the author's uncle, age - mid-30s. (courtesy of Argonne National Laboratory).

The Met[allugical] Lab, Manhattan Project, Site B, University of Chicago.

"Site B was described by one employee as 'a pretty disreputable building, but it also had an assortment of guards, with pistols strapped to their belts.'" A former bottling plant for a brewery with stables in the back, Site B was the home of much early Met Lab research. Located at 61st and University Avenue near the south end of the Midway Plaisance, it housed under one roof a variety of researchers working on metallurgy, chemistry, and biology, as well as carpenters, shops, metal workers, a forge, and other equipment and support groups."*
William P. Norris, Division of Biological and Medical Research, Argonne News, May 1971.
Courtesy Argonne National Laboratory.

"New Chem[istry].", Manhattan Project, Site, University of Chicago. This is the building where my mother worked as a secretary and my father met Charles Coryell, who recruited him to the Project [See Chapter 7.].

"Critical work for the Met Lab was done at "New Chem," built quickly at the University of Chicago shortly after the start of the Manhattan Project." Courtesy Argonne National Laboratory.

United States of America
WAR
DEPARTMENT
ARMY SERVICE FORCES ~ CORPS OF ENGINEERS
Manhattan District

This is to Certify that

ELLIS P., STEINBERG
University of Chicago

has participated in work essential to the production of the Atomic Bomb, thereby contributing to the successful conclusion of World War II. This certificate is awarded in appreciation of effective service.

6 August 1945

Henry L. Stimson
Secretary of War

Washington, D. C.

United States of America
WAR
DEPARTMENT
ARMY SERVICE FORCES ~ CORPS OF ENGINEERS
Manhattan District

This is to Certify that

ESTHER STEINBERG
University of Chicago

has participated in work essential to the production of the Atomic Bomb, thereby contributing to the successful conclusion of World War II. This certificate is awarded in appreciation of effective service.

6 August 1945

Henry L. Stimson
Secretary of War

Washington, D. C.

Manhattan Project certificates, the author's father and mother.

Atomic Bomb: Decision - Szilard Petition, July 17, 1945

A PETITION TO THE PRESIDENT OF THE UNITED STATES

Atomic Bomb: Decision - Szilard Petition,

Source: U.S. National Archives, Record Group 77, Records of the Chief of Engineers, Manhattan Engineer District, Harrison-Bundy File, folder #76.

On July 17, 1945, Leo Szilard and 69 co-signers at the Manhattan Project "Metallurgical Laboratory" in Chicago petitioned the President of the United States.

United States, moral and material, may hav
situation. Its prevention is at present the so
virtue of her lead in the field of atomic pov

The added material strength which this lea
restraint and if we were to violate this obli;
the world and in our own eyes. It would th
bringing the unloosened forces of destructi

In view of the foregoing, we, the undersigr
as Commander-in-Chief, to rule that the Ui
war unless the terms which will be impose
knowing these terms has refused to surrenc
to use atomic bombs
all the other moral re:

July 17, 1945

A PETITION TO THE PRESIDENT OF THE UNITED STATES

Discoveries of which the people of the United States are not aware may affect the welfare of this nation in the near future. The liberation of atomic power which has been achieved places atomic bombs in the hands of the Army. It places in your hands, as Commander-in-Chief, the fateful decision whether or not to sanction the use of such bombs in the present phase of the war against Japan.

We, the undersigned scientists, have been working in the field of atomic power. Until recently, we have had to fear that the United States might be attacked by atomic bombs during this war and that her only defense might lie in a counterattack by the same means. Today, with the defeat of Germany, this danger is averted and we feel impelled to say what follows:

Atomic Bomb:

Signers listed in alph

31. HERBERT
32. ALEXAND
33. RALPH E.
34. LAWRENC
35. ROBERT J(
36. NORMAN
37. GEORGE S
38. ROBERT J.
39. MARIETT/
40. ROBERT S
41. J. J. NICKS
42. WILLIAM
43. PAUL RAL
44. LEO ARTE
45. ALFRED P
46. ROBERT L
47. C. LADD P
48. ROBERT L
49. WILFRED
50. MARGARI
51. WILLIAM
52. B. ROSWE
53. GEORGE /
54. FRANCIS 1
54. ERIC L. SII

1. DAVID S. ANTH(
2. LARNED B. ASP!
3. WALTER BARTI
4. AUSTIN M. BRU
5. MARY BURKE, |
6. ALBERT CAHN,
7. GEORGE R. CAR
8. KENNETH STEW
9. ETHALINE HAR'
10. JOHN CRAWFC
11. MARY M. DAIL
12. MIRIAM P. FIN!
13. FRANK G. FOO
14. HORACE OWE!
15. MARK S. FRED
16. SHERMAN FRII
17. FRANCIS LEE F
18. MELVIN S. FRI!
19. MILDRED C. GI
20. NORMAN GOL!
21. SHEFFIELD GO
22. WALTER J. GR!
23. CHARLES W. H
24. DAVID B. HALI
25. DAVID L. HILL
26. JOHN PERRY H
27. EARL K. HYDE
28. JASPER B. JEFF
29. WILLIAM KAR'
30. TRUMAN P. KC

http://www.dannen.c

The war has to be brought speedily to a successful conclusion and attacks by atomic bombs may very well be an effective method of warfare. We feel, however, that such attacks on Japan could not be justified, at least not unless the terms which will be imposed after the war on Japan were made public in detail and Japan was given an opportunity to surrender.

If such public announcement gave assurance to the Japanese that they could look forward to a life devoted to peaceful pursuits in their homeland and if Japan still refused to surrender our nation might then, in certain circumstances, find itself forced to resort to the use of atomic bombs. Such a step, however, ought not to be made at any time without seriously considering the moral responsibilities which are involved.

The development of atomic power will provide the nations with new means of destruction. The atomic bombs at our disposal represent only the first step in this direction, and there is almost no limit to the destructive power which will become available in the course of their future development. Thus a nation which sets the precedent of using these newly liberated forces of nature for purposes of destruction may have to bear the responsibility of opening the door to an era of devastation on an unimaginable scale.

If after this war a situation is allowed to develop in the world which permits rival powers to be in uncontrolled possession of these new means of destruction, the cities of the United States as well as the cities of other nations will be in continuous danger of sudden annihilation. All the resources of the

http://www.dannen.com/decision/45-07-17.html   1/29/2003

56. JOHN A. SIMPSON, JR., Physicist
57. ELLIS P. STEINBERG, Junior Chemist
58. D. C. STEWART, S/SGT S.E.D.
59. GEORGE SVIHLA, position not identified [Health Group]
60. MARGUERITE N. SWIFT, Associate Physiologist, Health Group
61. LEO SZILARD, Chief Physicist
62. RALPH E. TELFORD, position not identified
63. JOSEPH D. TERESI, Associate Chemist
64. ALBERT WATTENBERG, Physicist
65. KATHERINE WAY, Research Assistant
66. EDGAR FRANCIS WESTRUM, JR., Chemist
67. EUGENE PAUL WIGNER, Physicist
68. ERNEST J. WILKINS, JR., Associate Physicist
69. HOYLANDE YOUNG, Senior Chemist
70. WILLIAM F. H. ZACHARIASEN, Consultant

Source note: The position identifications for the signers are based on two undated lists, both titled "July 17, 1945," in the same file as the petition in the National Archives. From internal evidence, one probably was prepared in late 1945 and the other in late 1946. Signers were categorized as either "Important" or "Not Important," and dates of termination from project employment were listed in many cases. It is reasonable to conclude that the lists were prepared and used for the purpose of administrative retaliation against the petition signers.

http://www.dannen.com/decision/45-07-17.html   1/29/2003

Petition from scientists at the Met Lab in Chicago urging President Truman to not use the atomic bomb on Japan since the war was over with Germany. Signer No. 57, Ellis P. Steinberg.

Entrance to the Tech Area, Los Alamos. Special passes were required to go past this gate. Spouses and children of scientists and engineers were not allowed inside. Courtesy of Los Alamos Historical Society Archives

Badge from the War Department Army Navy Production award at Elwood Ordnance Plant, Kankakee, Illinois

Envelope sent to my father with "address" of the Los Alamos laboratory during the war–P.O. Box 1663, Santa Fe, New Mexico and postmark from the Oak Ridge, Tennessee laboratory postmarked from Knoxville, Tennessee.

The badge photo of Dana M. Mitchell
(Dana D. Mitchell's father) from Los
Alamos during the Project. Courtesy of
Los Alamos Historical Society Archives

The badge photo of William A.
Higinbotham (Julie Schletter's father)
from Los Alamos during the Project.
Courtesy of Los Alamos Historical
Society Archives

Trinity obelisk, on the site of the first atomic blast. The plaque reads, "Trinity site where the world's first nuclear device was exploded on July 16, 1945."

Women workers at a cesium-137 irradiation facility at Oak Ridge National Laboratory during the Project [postcard]. Cesium-137 is produced by the nuclear fission of uranium-235.

146

ATOM-SPLITTING IS JUST ANOTHER WAY OF CAUSING AN EXPLOSION.

To begin with, you must realize that atom-splitting is just another way of causing an explosion. While an atom bomb holds more death and destruction than man has ever before wrapped in a single package, its total power is definitely limited. Not even hydrogen bombs could blow the earth apart or kill us all by mysterious radiation.

YOUR CHANCES OF SURVIVING AN ATOMIC ATTACK ARE BETTER THAN YOU MAY HAVE THOUGHT.

Because the power of all bombs is limited, your chances of living through an atomic attack are much better than you may have thought. In the city of Hiroshima, slightly over half the people who were a mile from the atomic explosion are still alive. At Nagasaki, almost 70 percent of the people a mile from the bomb lived to tell their experiences. Today thousands of survivors of these two atomic attacks live in new houses built right where their old ones once stood. The war may have changed their way of life, but they are not riddled with cancer. Their children are normal. Those who were temporarily unable to have children because of the radiation now are having children again.

WHAT ARE YOUR CHANCES?

CLOSE TO THE EXPLOSION, YOUR CHANCES ARE ONLY ONE OUT OF TEN.

If a modern A-bomb exploded without warning in the air over your home town tonight, your calculated chances of living through the raid would run something like this:

Should you happen to be one of the unlucky people right under the bomb, there is practically

4 "Modern" atomic bomb, as used in this booklet, refers to the "nominal" bomb described in the "Effects of Atomic Weapons," published in June 1950 by the Atomic Energy Commission.

From the pamphlet Survival Under Atomic Attack, Distributed by Office of Civil Defense, State of California, The Official U.S. Government Booklet, October 1950.

no hope of living through it. In fact, anywhere within one-half mile of the center of explosion, your chances of escaping are about 1 out of 10.

On the other hand, and this is the important point, from one-half to 1 mile away, you have a 50-50 chance.

From 1 to 1½ miles out; the odds that you will be killed are only 15 in 100.

And at points from 1½ to 2 miles away, deaths drop all the way down to only 2 or 3 out of each 100.

Beyond 2 miles, the explosion will cause practically no deaths at all.

Naturally, your chances of being injured are far greater than your chances of being killed. But even injury by radioactivity does not mean that you will be left a cripple, or doomed to die an early death. Your chances of making a complete recovery are much the same as for everyday accidents. These estimates hold good for modern atomic bombs exploded without warning.

WHAT ABOUT SUPER BOMBS?

Do not be misled by loose talk of imaginary weapons a hundred or a thousand times as powerful. All cause destruction by exactly the same means, yet one 20,000-ton bomb would not create nearly as much damage as 10,000 two-ton bombs dropped a little distance apart. This is because the larger bombs "waste" too much power near the center of the explosion. From the practical point of view, it doesn't matter whether a build-

Suited up after the Trinity blast. Courtesy of Los Alamos Historical Society Archives

Photo of Bikini Atoll wrapped in unlabeled brown paper; found in my father's closet when my mother was moving from the house I grew up into a retirement community.

The Little Mermaid – My favorite place in Copenhagen when I was five while my father was working at the Niels Bohr Institute – University of Copenhagen, Denmark. Guggenheim Fellowship

Niels Bohr Institute, Copenhagen, Denmark

I would feel so blessed to glimpse the Dama dama, the white fallow deer on our way to the lab. They lived in the Waterfall Glen Forest Preserve that completely surrounds Argonne National Laboratory, DuPage County, Illinois. Courtesy of Argonne National Laboratory

Inside the cyclotron at Argonne National Laboratory, Argonne, Illinois. Courtesy of Argonne National Laboratory

Aerial view of the cyclotron, now the Advanced Photon Source (APS)– Argonne, Illinois. Courtesy of Argonne National Laboratory

Department of State
OF THE
United States of America

To all to whom these presents come, greeting:

This is to certify that ELLIS P. STEINBERG

has been designated an Adviser on the United States Delegation to the

International Conference on the Peaceful Uses of Atomic Energy to be held

at Geneva, Switzerland, August 8 to 20, 1955.

FOR THE SECRETARY OF STATE:

Harold J. Kissich
DIRECTOR, OFFICE OF
INTERNATIONAL CONFERENCES

WASHINGTON, D. C.,

August 8, 1955
DATE

Geneva conference certificate, Peaceful Uses of Atomic Energy, 1955.

Ellis P. Steinberg (the author's father) at work at his lab at the Nuclear Physics Division, Argonne National Laboratory, Argonne, Illinois (1960s).

Ellis P. Steinberg at work (1980s).

Chapter 17

Dana D. Mitchell

*It is twenty minutes before midnight on a June night in
2005. Dana D. Mitchell, son of Dana P. Mitchell, Assistant
Director to Robert Oppenheimer at Los Alamos Lab, and
I are sitting on a maroon carpet in the hallway off the
lobby of the Doubletree Hotel in Oak Ridge, Tennessee. We
met yesterday after the talk he gave on being a child at
Los Alamos during the war. It has been a long day at the
60th-anniversary observance of the Manhattan Project,
which included a talk by Paul Tibbets—pilot of the Enola
Gay that dropped the A-bomb on Hiroshima—and a tour of
Y-12 [an isotope-separation site that used the calutron, a
modification of the first cyclotron]. It is very late and we're
both tired, but Dana honors his agreement to meet with
me.*

*We are talking about what it's like to have a father
who worked on the Manhattan Project and to be raised by a
nuclear physicist.*

We're both slightly crazy, but that's what makes it fun. [We
share a laugh.] I would imagine it's somewhat different in
each of our situations. Subconsciously I associated a lot of
power with my father. I tried to always do what I thought my
father wanted and I did it pretty well.

Were you the oldest child?

I'm an only child.

My father was a good scientist and an excellent teacher. I really enjoyed him teaching me science. I think this mutual enjoyment caused my mother to feel left out sometimes. She often complained about that, and I used to get mad because I knew that she understood what we were talking about, but pretended she didn't. She refused to participate in our discussions.

Did I tell you that, when I was in high school, Paul, a buddy of mine, and I made a Wilson cloud chamber?[34] It even had Geiger counters hooked up so that it would trigger when a cosmic ray came by.

That's pretty cool.

Paul and I won in the Science Talent Search and went together to Washington, DC. After college, Paul worked his way up and eventually became president of a large high-tech firm based in Connecticut.

I was an overachiever trying to live up to my father and I was a real brain in high school. I actually placed fourth out of 22,000 entries. I shook hands with Harry Truman at the awards ceremony.

The most fun was after the Westinghouse Awards banquet when we were on our way home, and all the kids exploded into this Pullman train-car for the trip back. I was standing in the vestibule of the car when the conductor came through. Seeing the storm of pillows flying between berths, he said, "Are you in charge of those kids in there?" I said, "Certainly not!" and ran off in the opposite direction.

Tell me about the jar you brought here to Oak Ridge.

I had some samples of the Trinity sand that we collected when my father took me to see the bomb site, so I thought I'd bring a jar of it to the reunion. I thought if anybody wanted some, they'd be welcome to it.

Isn't that still somewhat radioactive? You just took it on the plane? I mean, you do realize it is post-9/11. [Ignoring my comment, Dana continues].

It is very stark to pull the jar out and see this sand that was turned into green glass, trinitite. It has all these red stains in the glass where the tower had been vaporized. The vaporized iron combined with the silicon dyed the glass blood red. I carry that sort of thing with me to help people appreciate what a nuclear bomb can do.

We both carry that with us in different ways.

My father said that his main reason for wanting me to see the Trinity test site was to be able to remind people of the seriousness of a nuclear weapon. I was convinced, and traumatized, by this evidence that the A-bomb is real, extremely serious, and can do horrible damage.

My father wanted me to pass my fear and respect for the power of the bomb to anyone who would listen. I feel that part of my mission is to tell my Trinity story whenever I can. I also support the Nuclear Threat Initiative[35] and what they are doing to lock down all the Russian nuclear materials.

Where did you go to school?

I went to Columbia University because it was free. My father was a professor there and, according to him, you couldn't get a better education than at Columbia. I believe the real reason was that my mother wanted to keep me close to home and under her thumb. I think also that my father wanted me to win the Nobel Prize that he never won.

My father was also very disappointed he never won the Nobel Prize. Unfortunately, neither your father nor mine realized that is quite a burden to pass onto your children.

Columbia was a tough school, and I majored in a tough subject—physics. In some ways I enjoyed the humanities more; but physics was fascinating. For me, trouble came when I went to graduate school. I hit a learning block. This was after I decided that the math I needed to get a Ph.D. in physics was beyond me. I liked physics instrumentation, so I inquired and became an engineer.

I had trouble in graduate school with major learning blocks. I couldn't get my brain to work. It turns out that is not uncommon with kids who have high-achieving parents. In my case, after some years of therapy, it was pretty much attributed to the fact that I was extremely afraid of my father and didn't want to compete with him on any level.

I know that phenomenon very well.

I thought that if I got a Ph.D. like he did, I'd be dead in the water. So this was something to be avoided at all costs, and I did avoid it. I never got a Ph.D. I have friends, both leaders in their scientific fields, whose sons had a terrible time getting a degree. Right now, one of them works in a clothing store. He is trying not to flunk out of college. Another friend is an astrophysicist, and his son is a basket case. I tried to convince them all that this could be fixed. I didn't have any luck. It's still hard to get people to think going to therapy is okay. I just talked to him a few days ago and I'm feeling bad about his situation.

It took me dropping out of college three times to finally

graduate. I had major learning blocks, both thinking I could not do anything intellectually and being afraid I would succeed. When I did succeed in something, on some deep level, I somehow equated it with the bomb.

I find, even now, that writing up my Los Alamos experience is not easy. I've done some, but the process crawls along.

I completely relate to that. In your talk you said you spent three years in Los Alamos. What ages were you?

I lived there from age ten to twelve. My father was a nuclear physicist but was recruited by Oppenheimer to head up purchasing at Los Alamos, because he needed someone who would know what the project needed before they knew it themselves and then go out and buy it. Although his responsibilities were essentially those of a purchasing agent, Oppenheimer made him an assistant director and a member of the governing board. He had the comprehensive overview of the project that he needed to do the job.

My dad told me they were spending about a million dollars a day—$13 million in today's money—and it took about 340 people under him each day to spend it. It's not that easy to spend a million dollars a day and it had to be done secretly. They set up remote purchasing offices. One was in Denver, and all the calls went through an army-intelligence switchboard, so it looked like they were actually coming from Denver, when they really originated in Los Alamos.

Sometimes extreme security was a real problem.

The Los Alamos lab had the highest purchasing priority in the country. They could pull something from anywhere. My father said that he tried to find out whose "mouth" the project was taking something out of. He had the judgment that if Los

Alamos's need was not nearly as important as another project's needs, he would not use the high-priority status. There was a lot to admire about my father. He was absolutely honest and scrupulous and wouldn't allow anybody to take any kind of gifts—no war profiteering.

Getting back to getting raised by a nuclear physicist, I dropped out of graduate school. I didn't really know what my problem was. I had been working summers in an oceanographic laboratory and they hired me as a full-time engineer. I spent the next ten years or so as an oceanographic engineer developing instruments for ships.

For the first several years, until I started therapy, I was unable to write a progress report. I could not pick up a pen; I could not write down what I had been doing—again, somehow, like I couldn't compete. I was doing good work but couldn't write about it. Fortunately, my boss was kind enough to just let me tell him what was going on.

You got farther than I did. I was the youngest. I saw my brother and sister become high achievers—straight A's, valedictorian, head of the debate team, and so on—and they still got yelled at. When I was a kid I saw this and thought, Why should I bother? I sort of gave up before I even started. It took me decades before I began to have a sense of belief in myself and my talents. In between the many attempts to complete college I had a long string of jobs: secretary, cab driver, cardiology technician, bus dispatcher, library assistant, and a bunch of others I don't even remember.

I was in my early thirties when I finally entered adolescence and evolved into my own person. At one point my mother had a psychotic break, so when she went into the Neuropsychiatric Institute, her psychiatrist interviewed me.

I asked him what I could do to get help for myself. He suggested a brilliant therapist and, with his help, I gradually got to the point where I could publish papers and give them at talks. I was even able to do public speaking and present them at meetings. For years I went around with very painful, perpetual tension headaches. One day they were gone! I thought, Wow, this is fantastic. Maybe therapy works.

Years later the Navy decided to combine Hudson Labs with the Naval Research Lab [NRL] in Washington, DC. They offered me a job. I knew how humid it was there and so I turned it down. Now I'm living near Annapolis, Maryland, where it can get very hot and humid.

These things happen.

I was consulting on teaching machines—sort of doctored film projectors—to show medical techniques; I then went full-time as vice-president with that company. Toward the end of the first year, I got suspicious that the company president wasn't telling me what was going on. I made a midnight raid on the books and found out that he was paying some of the salaries with money reserved for federal income-tax withholding. This really frightened me.

I had lunch with a family friend who was a business lawyer. He brought a tax lawyer along with him, and their advice was to get out before the IRS went after me personally for the missing taxes. So I left immediately. What a bomb.

You had your scruples.

Yes, but for the first time I was out of a job with nowhere to go. I remember going with my first wife, Lee, and our kids to Playland in Rye, New York. Suddenly it dawned on me, "What am I doing here, having fun, when I don't have a job?"

I looked at ads in the New York Times and responded to one from Columbia University's Nevis Laboratories. When I interviewed, the chief engineer and I clicked. I spent the rest of the afternoon working with him on a design problem.

So you were back at Columbia University.

Yes. I worked at Nevis for a while making nuclear-physics instrumentation. Then I was assigned to making instruments for sounding rockets that the Astrophysics Lab at Columbia was flying. These projects had hard NASA deadlines that put me in direct competition with the nuclear physicists.

Back to that conundrum.

By that time, I'd had enough therapy to be assertive enough to handle the situation—as a matter of fact, there were some complaints about me being too pushy.

One day the head of the Astrophysics Lab came in and said that we were going to form our own engineering group. He wanted me to head it up and hire all the employees. I was able to assemble an excellent group of people. That job was extremely interesting. When I was doing oceanographic instrumentation I noticed that the challenges of low-power, limited room, and high performance were similar to the challenges of designing instruments for space. Now I had a chance to meet this new challenge. Furthermore, I liked going down to White Sands for rocket launches. But I never went to the Trinity site when I was there.

[I didn't think to ask Dana at the time if he felt nervous about going back to see the site or if it was just not feasible to go there at the time.]

The Astrophysics Lab received money to make satellite instruments. We built these instruments from scratch to full

NASA reliability standards for the Orbiting Solar Observatory (OSO).

When I went to the Goddard Space Flight Center to be interviewed by the NASA OSO Satellite project head, I was alone in this conference room when the head of the project came in. He sat down across from me and said, "What the hell makes you think you can build a satellite instrument?" So I told him, and he said "Okay." That was the interview.

Well, it certainly seems at that point that you had regained your confidence.

From a psychological view, I had recuperated fairly well, especially in the realm of career. I didn't like people detailing everything I should do, so I became the boss. Of course, people still told me what to do, but I had more latitude.

After some of those projects were done I was talking with Jesse Mitchell—no relation [to me]—who was head of NASA, and he said that the space shuttle overruns were eating up huge gobs of NASA science money. He said, "I bought my farm in Virginia and I'm out of here." He told me to seriously think about leaving.

What did you do?

Two years before this happened, the University of Arizona Astronomy Department was setting up a research-engineering support group and asked me to head it up. My kids were still in high school, so I declined. But two years later I took the job and became Assistant Director of Steward Observatory.

Steward embarked on making the next generation of very large telescopes. Roger Angel and Nick Wolfe knew that researchers would need large "light buckets" to follow up with studies of the Hubble Space Telescope discoveries. They were aggravated by the complete lack of progress in large telescopes after the Palomar 200-inch was completed in 1948. They sat down and did the whole comprehensive systems design, right up to the final huge telescopes. This was the start of a new epoch. Among other things, it resulted in the making of huge short-focal-length, lightweight mirrors. Everyone said it couldn't be done! By huge, I mean if you stand them on edge they're larger than a two-story house—8.4 meters in diameter.

Getting back to what happened to the nightmare...

What nightmare?

When I was working at Hudson Labs I developed this new level of confidence and I felt that, in so many areas, I could do whatever was put in front of me and develop new avenues of research. I felt that spirit inside me of confidence, intellect, and creativity. I recognized that these fears I had of my father were quite irrational, almost.

I say almost, because when I was working at Hudson, the police came knocking at the door of my apartment, and said, "We want you to come to your parents' apartment with us." I should explain that, a year before, my parents had gotten an apartment across the driveway from us. It made us very uncomfortable. Among other things, they wanted to come over and see the kids at 10:30 at night. We had to say no.

To make a long story short, the police took me over to my parents' apartment. They said my folks were dead. The medical examiner was there and she said, "You are going to have to identify your parents, because that way you will know exactly what happened to them." The chief of police was there and strongly objected to subjecting me to that gory scene. The examiner insisted, so they led me into the bedroom where my mother was lying on the bed with a bullet hole in her forehead. She had bled out into the mattress underneath her. My father was lying on the floor with his blood and brains all sticking to the ceiling. They called it a murder-suicide.

Oh my God, Dana, how horrendous.

Fortunately, I was in therapy, but I just about started over. It was stunning, the worst thing that ever happened to me. It was horrifying and scary. Not just to me but to my whole family. My kids thought, if Granddaddy killed their grandmother, did this mean that daddy might kill them? They went into therapy along with the rest of us. I was furious with my father. If you ask how my children are doing, in my bitterness I might say: "Well, they had a glitch in the road."

I would guess so.

A year before this mayhem my folks slammed into a bridge abutment. The steering shaft of the car went through my father's chest and damaged his heart. He survived, although he looked dead when he got to the hospital. My mother had head injuries and kidney and liver damage. She couldn't remember anything or recognize me for three months. Her foot was severed and never reconnected right. They never recovered; and, a year later, he just decided to put an end to it. I still feel extremely damaged by it. On the bright side, the kids are doing better.

All that happened nearly forty years ago but is still very clear in my mind. I will not have guns in the house. When I see gratuitous violence on TV, I think that, when people watch these shows, they have no idea what it really looks like. I cleaned out their apartment. We got a cleaning crew in there first, but still, when I was cleaning out some things from his bureau I found a piece of his skull. I looked at it and I said to myself, "Oh yeah, honeycomb—that's skull."

It was absolutely the worst thing that ever happened to me.

I'm so sorry. I can't imagine.

But here I am. I would like to think neurotic, but reasonably sane.

Well, we are all neurotic.

Yes, I think so.

My conversation with Dana continued when, in the summer of 2008, we recreated the trip he took from Los Alamos to Trinity with his father at age twelve, just weeks after the first successful A-Bomb test. [See Chapter 19, Part 3.]

Chapter 18

David Seaborg

I wind my way across the San Francisco-Oakland Bay Bridge to the East-Bay suburb of Walnut Creek on a rainy winter day in 1998. I am on my way to meet with David Seaborg, the son of Glenn Seaborg—a prominent scientist on the Manhattan Project, a Nobel Prize winner, and the discoverer of plutonium and ten chemical elements, including element 106, seaborgium—Sg, the first element ever named for someone living. I am happy to see the windshield wipers of my budget rental car slapping rain back and forth, having just escaped a week in the ice, snow, and freezing temperatures of Wisconsin, where I live.

After driving past Oakland, through the Caldecott Tunnel that cuts through the East Bay hills, and into the upper-class communities of Orinda and Lafayette, I reach Walnut Creek, a suburb in the shadow of Mount Diablo. I am invited inside his small, but comfortable, living room in the condominium where David lives with his wife. I am offered herbal tea and learn that David is an avid environmentalist. I am admonished for driving and not taking the BART (Bay Area Rapid Transit) train. David tells me he is an evolutionary biologist and organizer and says he has had snakes, lizards, and frogs since he was a kid. Some are currently in cages on the living room floor. I share that

*my brother, also named David, had an anaconda when we
were growing up. Luckily it was kept in the garage.*

*We sit down to discuss memories of his father and fears
from his childhood pertaining to nuclear issues. I glance
warily at the very large snake in the cage next to me on the
floor as David begins.*

My mother delayed going to the hospital, so I was born on our
front porch and came out so fast I would have hit the front
porch, but my dad caught me. The doctor showed up, but was
too late. So I was born just before 11 p.m. on 4/22/49, which,
on my twenty-first birthday in 1970, became Earth Day.

You were in a hurry; you had a premonition.

I never thought of that.

Do you have siblings?

I have four siblings who are living. My brother Peter, who
was three years older, passed away. He died at fifty-one of a
heart attack. My sister Lynn Cobb is two years older and is a
clinical psychologist. My brother Steve is two years younger
and became a social worker. He became disillusioned and
went back to school to become a second- and third-grade
teacher and now loves his work. Eric is five years younger
than me and is a journalist. He recently wrote an autobiog-
raphy with and about my dad.[36] Dianne is the youngest, ten
years younger than me, and is a gardener.

*You all have very interesting careers, helping the earth
and people.*

Yes. One of the things I have done is put together a loose

coalition of environmental leaders and organizations in the San Francisco Bay Area called the "U-Turn Society," which is dedicated to making the U-turn from destruction of the earth to preservation and restoration and conservation of the earth. It addresses global environmental issues like rainforests, global warming, climatic change, destruction of the ozone layer, and nuclear-weapons proliferation. I'm also a poet and wildlife photographer and have won awards in both.

How interesting—me too, on both counts—but no awards yet. I have had some poems published and do a lot of nature photography. How was it for you to have such a famous scientist for a father?

Growing up under my dad I was more aware of the danger of nuclear war than the general public. Other people were worried, but it varied as to how much they repressed it. It was prominent in my consciousness, and I had moments of worry, even terror, about it actually happening.

I was a child when we lived in Washington, DC, and my dad was Head of the Atomic Energy Commission (AEC), which is now the Department of Energy and a cabinet level post. He was at the AEC from 1961-71 and had a chauffeur for himself and our family. My dad's main office was on H Street near downtown. There was another office at Germantown; they had it there so they could decentralize the department in case of a nuclear war. He served under Kennedy, Johnson, and Nixon, and was advisor to eight presidents. There were only a few people that served under both Democratic and Republican regimes.

Regimes; well, that sort of gives a good clue to your politics.

The government's plan was that, if one bomb destroyed the DC office, they had another one in Maryland. There was a bomb shelter where my dad and his family were to go if a nuclear bomb was dropped, and we were supposed to be safe there. I remember what a farce it was to think that we could get all the family together in a car the moment an A-bomb would explode over Washington. The chauffeur was to take us to Germantown after we were all together. It was a thirty-mile, forty-five-minute drive from our house under ideal traffic conditions.

Can you imagine how it would be under those conditions? If we were somehow able to get to the shelter in time, Washington, DC, and Germantown would have been targets. The chances that people in that area would survive a direct hit was slim. If we did survive, everything above ground would be melted over and radiated when we ran out of food and water. I didn't know about nuclear winter then and that an all-out nuclear war would destroy the ozone. It would have been much worse according to the knowledge we have now, but I knew it was a big farce even then.

When do you first remember being aware that your father worked on the bomb?

I was a very young child, around five. I remember my father could do no wrong. I don't know if I had any awareness that he helped save us from Hitler and stopped the war. I remember, in my teens, he initiated the subject and said to me, "People ask me if I feel guilty about working on the nuclear bomb. The answer is no; I don't feel guilty at all. We knew Hitler was working on it and we were all worried and scared. We didn't know how far along he was and we needed to stop him."

The feelings I had on that were mostly supportive of what he said. Although nuclear weapons are so heinous, it's always going to be a little hard to know that your dad worked on something like that. At the same time, I really do understand the reasoning they had.

It took me a while to get to that point, but I understand it better now as well.

There was an incident that truly frightened me that was instigated by a speech at a rally at the University of California Davis during the Vietnam War. It was the night after Nixon mined Hanoi Harbor.

[*I remember solemnly watching the mounting numbers of American and Vietnamese dead and wounded on our black-and-white TV throughout my high school days. I close my eyes and can see Walter Cronkite reading the nightly news. Even though I did not know anyone who was in Vietnam at that time, I felt the widening gap between those who were there and those of us who opposed the war. As the numbers of Vietnamese dead surpassed the American casualties, the message seemed to be that we are winning the war—it won't touch you; it's a half a world away. But we did not win, and it did touch an entire generation. Looking back, it seemed I felt the effects of the Holocaust, the making and dropping of the atom bombs, and Vietnam as a continuum of destruction engulfing my far-removed Chicago suburban home.*]

Nixon had put up a blockade of the harbor, and the speaker seemed sure the Soviets were going to run the blockade. It turned out, of course, to not be true; but I believed the speaker. I don't know if he was trying to get people riled up, or was just misinformed, but I left the protest frightened that there would be a nuclear war. I called my Mom in Washington DC from Davis, California, where I was at school and asked her to talk to Dad to try and convince Nixon to remove the blockade.

Amazing. That's having connections.

Well, Mom said to me, "I won't do that. Your father has spent a lot of time and effort working for peace. I don't know why you are worried now?" I didn't get anywhere with her. I went to the student ticket window where they sold airline tickets and decided right then to buy a ticket to Australia. The agent looked at me strangely and said, "Why do you want to go to Australia?" I told him, "I think there is going to be a nuclear war and that's the last place it is going to come."

Whenever I hear about Australia and nuclear war I hear the slow, sad, soulful song "Waltzing Matilda" playing inside my head.[37] *I think we have been conditioned, at least in our generation, to associate the book and movie* On the Beach *with the end of the world by nuclear annihilation.*

That's true. So, anyway, the ticket agent said to me, "Buddy, if that happens, it isn't going to make any difference where you are." I knew he was right. The radiation would be in the food, air, and water, and everyone would die. It would just be a matter of time. So I stayed and, luckily, there was no running of the blockade and no nuclear war."

[In 1972, a few weeks before he ordered a major escalation in Vietnam, President Nixon told Henry Kissinger, "I'd rather use the nuclear bomb." Kissinger said, "That, I think, would just be too much." Nixon said, "The nuclear bomb. Does it bother you?" Then he said, "I just want you to think big, Henry."][38]

The other incident I remember very clearly was when I was a graduate student at the University of California Berkeley. I was renting a room from a family and woke up one night in a state of terror. I thought a nuclear war had begun. I looked out the window and part of San Francisco appeared to be gone. In the state I was in I didn't realize that, with the darkness, the fog, and Angel Island being between where I lived in Berkeley and the city, I couldn't see the San Francisco lights.

I thought, Oh my God, it's happened! Even before I looked toward the city I heard sirens and thought it was a nuclear warning signal. I was in a partly nightmarish, but awake, state and I called the operator.

The operator? Really?

Yes, I wanted to ask her if there had been a nuclear war. I was too embarrassed to ask her directly so I said, "Is everything all right?" She said, "Everything is fine, sir."

Do you remember what your dream was about?

No. I don't even think I dreamt about nuclear war. I think I was in some twilight-zone state, worried, and envisioning nuclear war.

Theta waves, hypnogogic hallucinations—just in Stage-1 sleep. Do you remember what year that was?

It was the first year I was a graduate student, so it was 1972-73.

That sounds really scary.

What were some of the other positions your dad held?

My dad worked at Lawrence Berkeley National Lab (LBL) and was Associate Director there for many years. That is where he made most of his discoveries of new elements in the Periodic Table. They named seaborgium in his honor, which was a bigger honor to him than the Nobel Prize.

[Seaborg was the principal or co-discoverer of ten elements: americium, curium, berkelium, californium, einsteinium, fermium, mendelevium, nobelium and element 106, seaborgium, named after him while he was still living.][39]

He also discovered more than 100 atomic isotopes and he developed the extraction process used to isolate the plutonium fuel for the second atomic bomb. But his most important discovery, plutonium, was made at the Metallurgical Lab in Chicago.[40]

That's where my father and uncle were. My mother talked about being friendly with your parents.

My dad signed the Franc Report, the petition asking the president not to drop the bomb on Japan. The signers wanted to drop a demonstration bomb in hopes the Japanese would surrender—seeing the destruction of what the bomb could do—rather than killing innocent civilians. To his death he defended his decision to support a demonstration bomb. He worked for years against nuclear weapons. As chairman of the Atomic Energy Commission under Kennedy he was instrumental in giving us the limited nuclear-test-ban treaty, which stopped testing nuclear weapons in the atmosphere. All the testing afterwards was underground. The limited test-ban was signed by the Soviet Union, the United States, and the United Kingdom in 1963. The Comprehensive Nuclear Test Ban Treaty [CTBT, signed by the U.N. General Assembly 9/10/96 but not ratified by eight nations] banned all nuclear military and civilian testing. My dad also lobbied for years, and it was finally ratified under Clinton. Of course, the

Congress hasn't ratified that treaty; we have stopped the testing underground. His testimony in Congress and his negotiations with the Soviets helped get it through. Without his help we wouldn't have gotten it, at least not that early.

My father discovered 80% of the isotopes used to diagnose and treat disease. He discovered more than 100 isotopes in all. Iodine-131 is interesting because the guy working on the isotope iodine in medicine was frustrated because it had too short of a half-life. He asked my dad for another isotope with a longer half-life and [my dad] said "How long do you want the half-life?" and he said, "About a week." My dad came back and said, "I got another isotope; iodine-131." The other man said, "How long is the half life?" and [my dad] said, "About eight days"; and the guy was floored.

What is interesting is that it was used to save his mother. She had thyroid disease and was treated with Iodine-131. These medicines are a good thing, but low-level waste from hospitals is a problem.

Were you affected by his work on the bomb—which has the potential to destroy the earth—while you are working to save the earth?

Yes, I was profoundly affected by his work on the bomb, and it led to me having a lot of passion and interest in the elimination of nuclear weapons and world peace. I am not only an evolutionary biologist but an environmental organizer. I work for the Foundation for Biological Conservation and Research and, under that, is the World Rainforest Fund which I founded. [The World Rainforest Fund is a nonprofit organization to save rainforests and promote biodiversity.]

Did your dad influence you in your profession?

My dad's excitement about science rubbed off on me. We talked about science and politics throughout my years of growing up. When he was chairman of the AEC, I met a lot of politicians. It was very stimulating. As an adult I went to Nobel Prize ceremonies; at the 90th many past winners were there that I met.

He won the Nobel Prize in 1951 when I was only two years old, so he was always famous during my life. I received a lot of reflected glory; doors were open to me. People would ask, "Are you Glenn Seaborg's son?" and would want to talk to me. The negative side was that people didn't recognize me for who I was. They would introduce me, "This is Glenn Seaborg's son." That is psychologically hard.

Fame is very enamoring; I saw my father admired and looked up to and saw the outward trappings of fame. It was a block to my career path as a scientist, an evolutionary biologist. I lost focus of the real reason to do science, which is the joy of discovery and the excitement at understanding the world. Science is exciting for its own sake, and I see it is as a spiritual practice.

I'd want to do a certain project because I thought it would get me famous and I would get sidetracked from what was real inner growth. It was very hard on me psychologically and took me away from the real, ultimately fulfilling, inward-seeking pursuits.

How do you look at science as being spiritual?

I don't mean religious.

I know.

This is my philosophy: science addresses very import-ant metaphysical questions, such as where did we come from, how did we get here? The Big Bang and chemical evolution and Darwinian evolution brought us here. Evolution also shows us that we are the genetic relative of bacteria, chimpanzees, plants, flowers, bees, insects, snakes—we all come from the same common ancestor. Ultimately we are all related and made of the same substance, which is DNA. The fact that science shows us that things are so deeply interrelated when we look at quantum physics and its concepts of non-locality— two things far apart, happening and affecting each other at the same instant in time, no time between them challenging the idea of cause and effect—is showing that everything is fundamentally interrelated. The tiger is our brother or sister because everything is interconnected. You can't destroy a forest without changing the climate and changing the capacity to grow food and affecting everything.

Therefore, most mutations are maladaptive or deleterious but, once in a while, because the organism is a system, the organism is changed and a mutation happens that causes a cascade effect; and you get positive feedback where one change in the organism leads to a change in natural selection which favors further change. Then you get very rapid change in the organism or the species.

My theory is that organisms are interrelated holistic systems; that a change or mutation in part of the organism— such as a fin of a fish or the wing of a bird—is usually disruptive. It upsets the balance in interplay of that organ or that gene with the rest of the system of the organism or the rest of the genetic system of the organism.

The Native American idea of reciprocity with respect to human relations and respect to nature is confirmed by scientific research and by the environmental crisis, which is something that is subject to scientific analysis. Relativity theory—[that] time and space are so fundamentally inter-related with mass and [that] time and space can be bent by mass—is another aspect where things are interrelated: the idea of purpose in the universe. Science, I think, confirms the more existential idea that there is no defined purpose in the universe, but we have to make our own: the uniqueness of the individual. Although we are all fundamentally interrelated, science also shows us that, because of our DNA, every individual is unique and special and important. The probability of any person's birth is so low, so improbable, that [it] is such a special thing that we are here. All this is what I mean by the spiritual aspects of science.

Maybe I've gotten more courageous in wanting a total elimination of all nuclear weapons. When I was younger I thought it was too much to ask to get rid of all nuclear weapons. I still believed at that time that some were needed for defense. I now think you don't need any of them. Although, politically, it's something I push for, [I] can't realistically hope that will happen.

My father was very supportive of my views and the efforts I have made for world peace and eliminating nuclear weapons. His support was very important to me because of who my father was and the work he did for peace.

For a while my father and I used to argue about nuclear power—he was for it; I was against it—but eventually I gave up on that. I figured he was not going to change. I was more of an environmentalist and wanted to put the rights of animals and nature equal with humans, realizing we are dependent on animals, plants, and the earth. My father always thought that humans came first, not recognizing that, if [we] destroy an ecosystem, it comes back to haunt us in terms of our ability to produce food and breathe clean air. He was an environmentalist, however, interested in saving land and advocated recycling.

My dad and I had debates in his later years about the programs of research going on at the Lawrence Livermore Lab and Los Alamos with regard to its nuclear stewardship program. The program is [expressly] to test if nuclear weapons are safe and reliable enough to simulate nuclear explosions.[41]

Its aim was to develop more powerful and effective nuclear weapons. My dad supported that on the grounds that, if you don't have that, you'll never get the Senate to ratify the comprehensive test-ban treaty. I disagreed with him about that. The Senate didn't ratify the comprehensive test-ban treaty anyway. I think they could have if Clinton had pushed for it more. I think we could have ratified it—that, of course, would have made my father's argument more cogent—but I think it's just a bad idea to have this program, which is really not only to keep nuclear weapons safe and reliable but to develop more, better weapons.

I agree. Switching focus, what stands out as a memorable conversation you had with your dad?

After his stroke I asked him if he wanted go on living. He was bedridden and in a wheelchair. He said, "I just want to live for your mom and you kids; otherwise, there is not much reason." My very last conversation with him [was] after he had come home from the hospital for the last time, after he decided he wanted life support suspended. He said he was in too much pain. I asked him what the worst thing I did was and he said, "You pulled up those flowers in the neighbor's yard across the street." I pulled up her pretty marigolds.

That's the worst thing he thought you did?

They brushed it off, as I was just looking for bugs, but I really did it just for fun. Isn't that funny, that he thought of that at the end? Then I asked what the best thing I ever did was. He said it was an article I wrote entitled, "A Rollercoaster Ride through the Nuclear Age," which was published in a book, *Learning to Glow.*[42]

What are your views on the state of the world today and the future?

I'm very pessimistic. We have between six to eight global problems that could bring down civilization. The destruction of the ozone layer is letting in ultraviolet light from the sun, which stunts the growth of forest and agricultural crops. We have global warming, with a scientific consensus that it is real and very serious. We are estimated to see somewhere between a seven-to nine-degree rise Fahrenheit over the next one hundred years. Only a two-degree decrease led to an ice age. There will be increased floods, droughts, greater forest fires. There have already been massive fires in the rainforests of Brazil, Africa, Mexico, and Indonesia, which led to widespread pollution of Southeast Asia a few years ago. We are losing our topsoil; we have six billion people [in 2001; 7.4 billion in 2016] doubling every forty years.

Russia almost accidentally launched a weapon on us, thinking we attacked them when a Norwegian satellite[43] was launched, and the Norwegians warned them as you always do when you launch a satellite. The Russian system was so disorganized that they didn't get the phone call, so they thought that they were under attack and they almost launched a nuclear weapon on us.

When was that?

A few years ago. They thought it was a launch from the U.S. sub when it was really a Norwegian satellite. I believe we are at greater risk of nuclear war than during the Cold War.

It certainly seems that way.

So if you add together all those factors, and unless we make some very radical changes now, we don't have much time left. I don't see that there is much hope left for civilization in fifty years.

That's all quite depressing.

Yes, I agree. On the other hand if we do nothing, there will be a time when it will be too late. We are not in the time when it is too late; we still have time to save it all. That is where I see the state of the world.

Do you think your views on the creation of the nuclear bomb have changed since you were a child?

I've had moments of anger at the whole idea of nuclear weapons just existing and, at times, I've been more philosophical about it. I have developed more of a desire to eliminate them all as I have matured.

The bomb was created in secret; there was so much that our fathers had to keep inside. What is your reaction to silence?

I have several responses to that. I had many colds in high school, and they led to tinnitus that led to ringing in my ears. That's why I wear this device that looks like a hearing aid. It has a constant shhhh sound. I have no loss of hearing, no pain, or loss of balance. So it is either the ringing or the shhhh sound. I never get to enjoy real silence.

In another way, silence comes when you can be in a

meditative state and be in tune [with] yourself. To grow internally is a much better life to seek than the external trappings of societal success. It's things and fame and money which this nation is destroying the earth over, because it's so out of touch with the inner life; and impressing the neighbors with useless things that are ultimately not fulfilling which you need some of to survive [in] only a minimal amount. So, in a sense, I prefer silence.

But I don't like silence with respect to the truth and nuclear weapons and my family background. I want to confront the truth and get in touch with what's real. It's only through being totally honest and open and seeking the truth like a scientist and doing it with integrity and talking the truth about myself that the truth can be seen; and, therefore, changes for the better can be made. Silence just keeps you in the same space and you never grow.

Chapter 19

Three Views of Trinity

⌇

One: Something from Nothing
Glen Klein

Glen Klein and I met at the Oak Ridge, Tennessee, Secret City Manhattan Project's 60th anniversary the same weekend I met Julie Schletter and Dana Mitchell. It was held June 16–19, 2005. Manhattan Project veterans, families, and even Paul Tibbets, pilot of the Enola Gay, were there, hosted by the Manhattan Project Heritage Preservation Association. Talks, discussions, and tours of K-25, the uranium-enrichment plant, took place. Glen came to the reunion with his father, John R. Klein, who at 16 had been the youngest person to work on the Project. Glen's home is in Phoenix, Arizona.

⌇

My father was a machinist at the University of Chicago [U of C]; they later transferred him to Los Alamos. He was a child genius, and in high school they put him into the U of C doing machine work. I don't know exactly how he skipped all his grades.

He was so young!

He worked at Los Alamos and was at the Trinity site when they tested the bomb. After the war he went back to the U of C and then Argonne National Laboratory. He left Chicago shortly thereafter.

My dad was in the metallurgical department. I'm glad he got out when he did. He was just lucky he didn't become sicker being around all those radioactive materials.

My father worked all his life at Argonne and began his career, like your father's, at the Met Lab. How did he end up going to Los Alamos?

Enrico Fermi requested it, and he had to ask my father's parents' [permission to] be his guardian; but he couldn't tell them where he was going or why. When [my father] turned eighteen he joined the Army. He always wore longer hair, combed back; he never got a haircut.

He was before his time.

They inducted him into the Army in five hours, and [he] didn't have time for a haircut.

What kind of work did he do at Los Alamos?

They were doing test work in one of the remote canyons called Payorita at Los Alamos—not on the mesa where most of the scientists were. A very small group made and built the components in scale shops. They also did the test firing.

Did your father talk to you much about his time at Los Alamos?

He told me that it had a profound impact on his life. He regularly talked about the fact that they were able to accomplish so much in a short amount of time and thought [of] everything he did there as an incredible experience. He conducted his business career with the concepts he learned working on the Project—any project that we worked on together would have to be done quickly. It was the way he did most everything and believed anything could be accomplished. He could build anything with minimal tools—essentially make something out of nothing.

Like the atom bomb.

On top of that it would have to be done right—perfection! It was hard growing up in those respects.

My father was like that too, a perfectionist.

What he pursued he didn't give up on until it was done—perfectly.

You mentioned that he was at the Trinity site when they tested the bomb?

Yes. They put him on evacuation detail to get him there; he was up at the front watching it.

Only a teenager; unbelievable. Did he have health problems that were related to that experience?

No cancer, but other health issues. He researched what happened to people in Japan and found he had non-cancerous radiation-exposure problems, same as they had—over-radiated throat area, which stops the saliva flow. He developed about nine different conditions that were related to his experiences at Los Alamos. He had a stroke about twenty-four years ago, an aneurysm. The effects of radiation can cause aneurysms, and a lot of things that happened to him were the results of over-radiation.

Did he talk to you about his feelings after the bomb was dropped and how they might have changed over time?

He was always positive about their accomplishment at Los Alamos. The actual dropping of the bomb was not something he discussed much. It was wartime, and they were trying to stop the war. That's why they put in the hours they did—to finish the Project and bring an end to the war.

What did he tell you about being at the Trinity test?

He said what affected him the most was the power of the blast. He had his back to it and he said it was brighter than daylight, incredibly bright. The light crossed in front of him, and he could see through his hands. An unbelievable amount of energy happened in that instant. That blast stuck with him the most: the pulse, then the blast, then the light.

I think it was greater than anyone ever anticipated it being. I don't think there is anybody still alive that was that close to the center of Trinity. There were very few people in the area—some were further out, but he was in the closest group. The amount of radiation that he was exposed to was astronomical. I have some declassified documents about how many rems they were exposed to. They didn't think it was bad at the time, but when they look at today's data, it is extremely significant.

Do you remember what the rems were?

I've got it on my computer, trying to get him disability benefits. They only gave disability for cancer and not the other medical problems that happened because of [the radiation]. One of the problems was that there weren't many people in his position to compare the effects of the exposure. There were only twelve people in his particular group. There were no statistics to go by, and he had to take information from the workers who were in other plants where there were thousands of people working.

Of course, that couldn't compare with what he was

exposed to. It amazes me that they got so close to the blast, knowing how powerful it could be.

That's not the only thing. They didn't have remote controls to work with radioactive materials in developing the machines; they weren't using any safeguards. They were directly exposed, handling it with their bare hands, whereas today you couldn't get within two miles of it. They were exposed to a lot of things before they really knew what the impacts were because it was so new; they knew it was dangerous but they didn't know how dangerous.

The next project my dad worked on was the fuel rods for the Schenectady, New York, SM-1 reactor in 1957; that was the U.S. first reactor that produced power.[44] That was another secret government project. It was kept very quiet. The first fuel rods went there, and the people that lived there would have been up in arms if they knew a reactor was in their backyard.

My father was involved with a lot of people in Los Alamos; he was one of the civilians in the scientific community so he was given a lot of access. He was in and out of Oppenheimer's office constantly. Consequently, another aspect of all this was that he was restricted to this country until the 1970s; he couldn't leave the United States.

Why was that?

I don't really know. I know he was watched that long, though. He always had to report his whereabouts. There were a handful of people who knew the entire process from beginning to end. I guess he knew too much. He wasn't with the Project any more so they kept tabs on him; our neighbors were always questioned.

That must have been nerve-wracking.

We were finally able to travel to Mexico in the 1970s.

Did you think they were keeping tabs on you?

I didn't know about it until later; he didn't share that with us. His big reason we didn't go to Europe was that he was afraid of flying. He gave that up until afterwards, and then he flew wherever he wanted.

Was it the FBI?

Yes. If he had to travel around the country, he had to report in at certain hours what his plans were.

But you didn't know anything about that when you were growing up?

Not at all. He didn't talk about any of that; it was just part of his life. When I got older I found out.

Was he angry about it?

No. After the stroke he was happy to be alive. He's always been an optimist. After the recovery from his stroke he's had a very positive attitude. You met him at the convention; he's smiling all the time.

Yes, I remember him well. Where did you live growing up?

I was born in Chicago and raised in Colorado. My father used to love going back to Santa Fe and Los Alamos. He loved the mountains—that's why he left Chicago; he didn't want to be there after experiencing life in Los Alamos. He always wanted to live in the mountains with lots of trees around. It's not something my mother wanted. She was a city girl but she went with him to live in the wilderness in Colorado. Where I grew up, the closest neighbor was five miles away.

Are you an only child?

No. I have one brother, two sisters.

Do you think they have similar views?

My dad didn't talk to them much. I was very close with my dad. He taught me and I had to teach my brother; my father didn't have patience with my brother. He didn't talk much with my sisters about his work either.

[We moved on to talk of Glen's views of the bomb and the development of nuclear weapons.]

First, I look at it that it saved a lot of lives. I don't look at it as negative. I look at all the things that we take for granted in our society that came out of the Manhattan Project. Testing the various scale models of the bomb was all done through coaxial cable; that's why it was originally developed. Television— something everyone watches—comes through a coaxial cable. Teflon, Plexiglas, and acrylic were also all developed for the Project. Pieces were put together with acrylic screws so that they didn't conduct electricity. Everything that came out of that short period of time created tremendous advances in science.

The next step was going to be harnessing the atom for peaceful purposes after the war was over; that was where everyone was going. It didn't turn out quite that way, however, but I see those developments as being positive— the same as what NASA has developed for the space program. When you have those types of projects, the benefit to mankind is great. When you look at it as billions of dollars to just stand on the moon, it doesn't look very good; but if you look at all the scientific advancements that helped us in our lives, it's a small price to pay. I never looked at the Project in a negative light. I'm sorry people had to die; but, at the same time, thousands of Americans were dying in the war. If Germany had the bomb, the United States would have been hit; it was just a matter of trying to end the war as fast as they could.

I think we are the most ridiculous country for not having more reliance on nuclear energy. We wouldn't have ever been in a position to depend on foreign countries for any of our energy needs if we had developed a strong nuclear-power program. I'm very disappointed in how the United States has handled the nuclear situation.

Nuclear weapons and the Cold War are something I grew up with. It's something you don't want to think that might actually happen. I think we need to continue to develop them; I believe staying stagnant is very dangerous. We have to continue to advance, as we did at the turn of the century or in the 1920s or 1950s.

I think we have enough nuclear weapons. Why develop a whole new set of them?

Because other people are developing them; every other country is going ahead with it. The biggest problem we have is letting the general public know what's going on as much as what we do. In my opinion, what goes on in defense is too open. Do you think we would have gotten as far with the Manhattan Project if it were broadcast on CNN? It never would have happened.

What is most striking to you about the Project?

The one thing that most amazed me was the grand scale of the Los Alamos section [and] seeing the size and scope of Oak Ridge, realizing that was all kept a secret and how fast the work was accomplished from concept to completion.

Putting it in today's terms, they wouldn't have even gotten an environmental-impact study to finish the foundation.

That's true enough. It was huge—all the sites spread out all over the country—and it was all a secret.

The sheer volume and enormity of the production and the sites to create that project [were] incredible. I look at the mechanical end of it—unbelievable; and, in those days, everything was done on a chalkboard.

No computers, no adding machines.

Slide rule, which was about it. My dad was a mathematical genius; until his stroke there wasn't a calculator that could calculate faster than he could. I think that's why Enrico Fermi had him working under him—because anything he could think of, my dad could build. The concepts they had he could put into a physical form. He was making lab equipment; he was the first one to do the tooling for beryllium that they used for the spacing of the fuel rods.

I think that's the hardest concept I have had to face in my life—what I accomplish compared to the accelerated pace that they were subjected to and worked under and how much they accomplished in a short period of time.

Yes, I know. I feel the same. I think about some projects I've worked on for years now and where have they gotten— this book, for example. They had so many people working together; it was their entire focus in life. They were isolated and had no other stresses on them. However, their families were neglected, especially the women and children who lived in Los Alamos during the war years. I am sure that is why my mother said no to moving there. She could see from a distance what it would mean.

I know. Just the group that my dad was with—the twelve people that were doing the final work—what they accomplished was unbelievable. There were smaller groups that they were working in; they enjoyed themselves. I have a photo album from Los Alamos; that's how he got into photography. He knew the photographer there and, somehow, he ended up with a good photo album. He was a supplying sergeant and, after eighteen months of the Army, he was a five-stripe G5 sergeant. Nobody goes up the rank that fast, but that's how he lived his whole life; whatever project he did he excelled in.

[I thought of how intimidated I was by my father's accomplishments, which seemed to extend to every area. He excelled in his field, receiving a Guggenheim Fellowship to work with Niels Bohr when he was only thirty-seven. He drew and painted and created beautiful scratchboard pictures, including one of Einstein's face fading into the universe. He played the clarinet and the violin. Beyond that, he excelled at tennis and golf. Kind of hard to live up to. I was brought back somehow and asked,] "What effect did that have on you?"

It was hard, but it's helped me in many areas of my life, like launching a product. It's frustrating dealing with people who don't know how fast something can be done.

How have you looked at the personal legacy of the bomb?

When everybody starting saying what we did to Japan, I knew what it did to members of my family. I keep it in perspective. There are different rules in wartime. You just wouldn't consider things happening in regular life like that, but [they do] happen. I look at the reality; look what happened in

Germany. There is a tremendous number of horrible events that happened all over the world at that time. I think the war created a high rate of accelerated knowledge and many things were developed that wouldn't have been otherwise. It's like computers twenty years ago; they were nothing to what they are today.

It's a hard thing, because it impacted my whole life growing up; it's the lifestyle we had that came from the impact on him as such a young person being a part of that Project. I think back to when I was sixteen; his involvement has definitely had an impact in my life. I was too naïve to know that too much was expected of me. The work ethic was he got very little sleep, generally working seven days a week: that's how I grew up.

Are you the oldest?

Yes.

Where is your dad now?

He lives in Arizona with my sister. He's taking care of his health—good diet. He takes better care of himself than I do. My dad has his room; he always had a nice house for the family but, for himself, he's never been one to have a lot. He's always stayed with the basics.

He got that from the Project.

He definitely got that from the Project.

I wish I had more of that.

I just got done building a couple of machines. I got rid of all my machine tools. I had to make some cattle benders and I put them together in my garage with very few tools. That's just the way I designed it, with what I had to work with. People were very impressed; they couldn't believe they were made in a garage. That's how I was taught to do things; do it with what you have and do it right.

"Perfection," a poem written by the author inspired by my interview with Glen, is at the end of this book in the section entitled **Interview-Inspired Poems.**

Three Views of Trinity

≈

Two: Serendipity
Julie Schletter

Julie Schletter's father, William A. Higinbotham, was an engineer in Los Alamos and a key co-founder of the Federation of Atomic Scientists (FAS) that was formed in 1945. He was the first FAS Chairman and FAS Executive Secretary and an official for fifty years.

FAS was a group of scientists from Los Alamos, Oak Ridge, and Chicago who felt an ethical obligation to bring their knowledge and experience to bear on critical national decisions, especially pertaining to the technology that went into creating the atomic bomb. Someone wrote her father a check for $500, and that got him started and through the next few months.

The FAS became a public-relations campaign, started by physicists as the "Bulletin of Atomic Scientists of Chicago." The aim of the Bulletin was to inform the public on nuclear policies and to advocate for international control of weapons. The Bulletin created the now-famous Doomsday Clock in 1947. It has moved closer and closer to midnight throughout the decades. As of 2016 it sets the time at three minutes to midnight.

Julie contacted me after seeing a request I'd posted on the Manhattan Project Preservation website hoping to interview "children" whose parents had worked on the project. She had just been looking through her father's papers, and her brother had directed her to the website. When I told her of the upcoming 60th anniversary Manhattan Project reunion, she found the timing auspicious, and we made plans to meet there.

On June 18, 2005, Julie and I met for lunch at the Blue Hound Café in the Jackson Square Historical Section of Oak Ridge, Tennessee, on the site of the original Town Center. Here, during the war years, Manhattan Project employees shopped, conducted business, and ate, all within a fence that kept their secret enclosed behind its gates. Even many who worked there only knew that they were working for the war effort. The Center in those days was open twenty-four hours a day, seven days a week, for someone was always at work at the labs. The Square today has a quaint atmosphere that allows glimpses into the wartime secret town of the 1940s.

Julie launched into her father's tale even before the waitress had brought us our first cups of coffee.

I mainly ignored my Dad's scientific accomplishments until after he died. What I most remember about him was he was a fabulous accordion player. He was a wild party animal. He could drink people under the table and sing all night long. He loved to stay up and party with anybody and everybody— young and old. He told jokes and stories and really listened when people spoke. He was empathetic and funny.

When my high school and middle school students would

come to school feeling down or crying, I'd say the same thing my dad said to me. "Are you unhappy more than half the time?" The answer would be no, I'm not unhappy more than half the time. So he would say, "So you're happy more than half the time?" "Yeah, I guess I'm happy more than half the time." He'd say, "You're doing better than breaking even, then. What do you expect? That's life." Then my students would chuckle just like I would when he said that to me. It was so wonderful; he was just that kind of guy.

[We both laughed, but as I reflected on her dad's advice I thought sadly of how my own mother would always say to my father, "You see the glass as half empty."]

Five years ago our annual family reunions began being mini-festivals. The dining room is always full of sheet music and instruments. People bring electric equipment and amplifiers, and we sing everything from church hymns, sea songs, folk songs, and great jazz, to some rock-and-roll. My cousin married a man who inherited all my dad's accordions, and it's almost like my father was reincarnated through Danny. He's a professional musician and he's the only person I've ever heard play, "I Can't Get No Satisfaction" on an accordion and you don't laugh. Mostly what I remember about my dad is his musicianship and partying.

My father played clarinet and violin. He played in the Argonne National Laboratory band, and every year they had a musical. I know them all because he would come home and practice all the songs: Damn Yankees, Carousel, *and* South Pacific.

I think music must have been a great release for an awful lot of them, and it continued throughout their lives.

Maybe they were reaching out to play the music of the subatomic spheres?

Considering all of our family music history I thought it was funny that, when in college I changed majors and told him I was going to change to music, he said, "Don't do it." I don't know why exactly. A group of us, however, put together a folk-singing group and we did a few songs like "The Night They Drove Old Dixie Down."

One of my favorites of The Band.

Up until the time of my dad's death in 1994 he was very active in his work. When he died, I was going through his papers, and there was some correspondence between him and Jeremy Stone, who was the current acting chairman of the Federation of American Scientists [FAS]. The annual meeting was in December, and they had already decided to rename the FAS building in Washington, DC after him. I called Jeremy Stone and told him Dad had died. He gave his condolences and wondered if he himself was going to make it to the dedication. He was very frail. He invited me and my family to accept the honor for the dedication on my dad's behalf. The meeting was held in the Senate building. Every Nobel laureate in science who was alive was there. Carl Sagan stood up and talked about my dad. That's really when I got my first clue that he might have been a little bit important. [We both laugh.]

I kind of knew he was a well-respected scientist because he would tell me things along the way, but it was always background information. He never bragged or said anything about how important he was. It was surprising—here were all these amazingly famous people talking about the wonderful things that he accomplished, such as [being] the first chairman of the FAS. Now there is a permanent plaque in Washington, DC, that honors him.

HIGINBOTHAM HALL
HEADQUARTERS OF FAS

WILLIAM A. HIGINBOTHAM (1910-1994)

1945, LOS ALAMOS: FIRST CHAIRMAN OF ALAS
1946, WASHINGTON: FIRST CHAIRMAN OF FAS
1946-47: FIRST FAS EXECUTIVE SECRETARY
1945-94: FAS OFFICIAL FOR A HALF CENTURY

OUR EFFORTS TO MOVE THE PLANET
REST ON THE FULCRUM HE FASHIONED

FEDERATION OF AMERICAN SCIENTISTS (FAS)

1994

*That's wonderful! [We walked down the tree-lined
street to my blue rented economy car and headed back to the
reunion's afternoon talks through the town that was built on
plutonium separation. On the drive back we continued our
conversation.]*

*My dad also got an award in 1987, luckily before he
died. It was the top award that year in Nuclear Chemistry
from the American Chemical Society in Denver. The whole
family went. They also honored him at the American
Chemical Society meeting in '93 after he passed away.*

Ah nice, so you had the same experience. When my
father died in November of 1994 at the age of eighty-four, the
whole family shipped to DC, and we arranged a memorial
out on Long Island for the Brookhaven Lab people and all
the neighborhood people. He had been ill for a while. I really,

really miss him. He was such a good influence on my life and so special. The memorial made me realize how important he was; I hadn't had a clue. A lot of it was yeah, that's my dad, and sometimes it was interesting.

Yes, I know. I felt the same way. I could never follow when he began talking of his work. My eyes would glaze over.

Afterward it became clear to me [about] his influence on the world. His scientific accomplishments and dedication to stopping nuclear weapons were enormous. When I realized this is when I decided I had to write a book.

My brother has collected some of his work in Dad's unique handwriting, and I've been collecting his memoirs. They, of course, didn't have spell-check back then; he was a terrible speller, really horrible!

No spell-check; they didn't even have adding machines.

I know, I know.

Slide rules, that's it.

I know. It's insane.

How could they figure out the science of it all? But then again, look at what they were able to accomplish. It boggles the mind.

It was incredibly primitive technology, which is why a lot of people didn't think it was going to work. First of all, they had unlimited funds; they could do anything. They were true visionaries and thought that anything could be accomplished. They thought, let's just give it a try.

Dana [D. Mitchell], subject of Chapter 17 the next interview, said his father had to spend a million dollars a day. They were young and not distracted by realities that would stop the creative scientific flow. Ironically, there was a war fueling the Project.

Speaking of primitive technology, one of the things my dad described in his memoirs was the day of the Trinity test. He was not planning to be at the test. He was writing reports and finishing things up when he got a frantic call from Oppenheimer, who told my dad that they needed a radio—right away.

My dad described the radio that they had at the site as putting out only one watt of power from batteries the size of a stable. They had extremely primitive transistors.

Here they can make this atomic weapon but they don't have working batteries? I can't believe...

I know. They've got this radio going—they only have to have something that works over eighteen miles—and they can barely hear each other. What is going on here? So he saves the day and brings out a workable radio.

So there he was at Trinity, standing next to the tower at Alamogordo, sunscreen on his face.

Sunscreen?

Yes, a bit inadequate.

Oh, just a bit.

He said on the four-to-five-hour bus trip back to Los Alamos, several people had pulled out bottles of scotch. They sat on the bus in silence; they passed bottles around and no one spoke the whole way.

I believe that is the night that my father knew that this would end the war early, but also that it was a horrible, horrible thing. It was around that time, I believe, that he decided to devote his life to the peaceful use of atomic energy. He conducted research, did politicking and schmoozing and flew all over the world. He went to South America, the Soviet Union, anywhere he could to promote the work of the scientists who wanted to stop the future production of atomic weapons.

His favorite thing to do—and my father could have done anything in the world—would have been to play with electronics. He would have created bigger and better computers. As a matter of fact, he created the first computer game— *Tennis for Two*—on October 15, 1958 at Brookhaven Lab in New York. But that is not how he wanted to be remembered.

So if Oppenheimer hadn't called him for the radio he never would have seen the test and the rest may never have happened. It was as if he was there so he could witness the explosion and know he had to bring to the world the opportunity to turn it around.

Of course, being from a psychology background my perspective is seeing is believing. Change can happen, but there is nothing like first-hand experience; and I think that was so important.

He described the test to me on any number of occasions, how horrifying it was—beautiful, strange, very amazing, but ultimately just horrifying. I have great recollections of that but I had no idea that he wasn't one of the people who were scheduled to be there at the test. But life is full of accidents, isn't it?

Maybe they are accidents; maybe not.

You're right. Serendipity, that gray area. I'm a great believer in it. Meeting you is a great example: why is it I dug up my father's stuff out of storage after ten years? I had no idea.

A few months ago my brother starting reviewing my dad's research; he's the caretaker of the documents in the family. He sent me the Manhattan Project site on the computer. I saw your ad, got in touch with you and a few other people, and I thought this could be my chance— serendipity, a gift.

I think you have to be attuned to it.

Have your antennae up.

Yes, well it's always there.

You just have to have the wires working.

Like a radio that was taken to Trinity.

So if you say, was your father guilty or did he feel guilty? he would say no, it was the right thing to do at the time. We had to do it. We thought we were in a race against the Germans. He believed that we probably ended the war against Japan. But he devoted the rest of his life to not having it happen again.

Later that day Julie and I met and talked again. Dana Mitchell had spoken that afternoon and I had met him the day before.

I was really interested in Dana's story of going out to the test site with his dad.

Yes, wasn't that fascinating? I'd like to go out there sometime.

Me too, but I don't think there's anything to see. I've seen pictures—the test site is all just sand. They have a monument. But what Dana saw, God!

He's got the remnants in a jar, small pieces of the trin-itite, the green glass that he and his father took back to Los

Alamos with them just weeks after the blast at Trinity.

Really, he kept all that?

He kept it.

Three Views of Trinity

~

Three: On the Road to Trinity
Dana D. Mitchell

In the summer of 2008 I asked Dana—the son of Dana P. Mitchell, Assistant Director to Robert Oppenheimer at Los Alamos Lab—if he would like to meet me in New Mexico to visit the Trinity site. We planned to recreate his trip from Los Alamos to Trinity when he was just twelve. His father was in his early 30s when he took Dana just weeks later to see the results of the successful test of the first atomic bomb.

On October fourth, Dana, his wife Vee, and I waited at the high school parking lot in the southeast New Mexico town of Tella Rosa. [It is currently (in 2016) open only one weekend every year to the public.] We were lined up in a caravan of around one hundred fifty trucks, cars, and SUVs on our way to the White Sands military base. At one end of the parking lot stood booths selling sodas, hot dogs, coffee, and water—somewhat reminiscent of the 4th of July or a high school football game.

I surveyed the others gathering there and wondered with interest and a bit of trepidation, why are they here? Is it general historical curiosity? Do some have a personal connection to the site like Dana and me? Is this just another tourist site in America? While we were waiting to drive into the site I talked to some of them. One man had been an Airborne Ranger and Special Forces Green Beret in Vietnam and was curious to see the site because of its historical significance. Another was in the Navy stationed on the Enterprise, *the first nuclear carrier. He said his dad had been in WWII off the coast of Japan and had wanted to see Nagasaki after the bomb was dropped, but hadn't been allowed to. Interestingly, his wife had worked as a secretary at the Met Lab in Chicago, but neither she nor my mother remembered each other.*

It was quiet inside the car. Dana and I were ready; I was not sure how Vee felt. I wondered about the desire to see and experience the dark reaches of the human mind and soul and the belief that we can survive the path to nuclear annihilation—a path that began at the spot where we would soon arrive. It was a strange comfort to think that perhaps the next generation might get it right. It was also a huge disappointment to me to know that every generation goes through this process. The songs "The Universal Solider" by Buffy Sainte-Marie and "Where Have all the Flowers Gone" by Pete Seeger played in my head as we slowly headed down the road into the military base.

We lined up for our single-file drive through the base to the Trinity site, escorted in by an official military security attaché. We were on our way to the spot that defined my parent's generation, driving backward in time to this desert site and its one and only historic event—a nineteen-kiloton explosion creating heat 10,000 times hotter than the sun—an unsettling legacy for my own and all future generations. The nuclear age hangs like an invisible shadow in our minds, in our politics, in our hearts, and as a spiritual tearing apart of the atom, which is really 99.99% empty space, and the smallest unit of matter. A fight against evil, a victory over Hitler and German fascism that engulfed the East with the destruction of two Japanese cities.

We were now inside the White Sands missile range. Dana almost vibrated with excitement at being back at the site, tempered with his years of personal exploration and reflection, and I could see the sadness in his eyes.

~~~

The last time I was at Trinity was when I was twelve years old, just after the first atomic bomb test. I've been trying to place the time when my father wrangled passes for us to go to the test site. I was trying to remember from the temperature exactly when that was. I remember being on a long stretch of highway, like we are on now, but it was when cars didn't have air conditioning, so we could really feel the heat—continuous blasts of hot air as we went mile after mile in the middle of nowhere.

We arrived at a clapboard wood guardhouse, nothing fancy, outfitted with a small tower for the FM radio antennae connecting together the guardhouses and radio-equipped cars. Outside the house was a solider sitting there under an umbrella to keep the sun off.

There was a car maybe every few hours and the guard seemed very bored, just saying hello, goodbye, safe trip or something like that. He said he would radio ahead to the next guard station and tell them we were coming. Then it was back to the soldier's boredom and our monotonous motoring through the desert scrub.

How long did it take to drive to the site?

Forever! It was a long, dull, slow ride through the desert.

What were your father's reasons for taking you to the site so soon after the test?

Before we left, my father told me he wanted me to understand why he was going to be spending a lot of time in Washington, DC, meeting with different congressional representatives and senators, people in government lobbying for civilian control of atomic energy and atomic weapons. Indeed, for a little while they managed to have civilian control.

Really? I never heard of that. [See index for an article on civilian control of atomic weaponry.][45]

Eventually the military got hold of it and convinced everybody that they were the ones to handle the whole thing, unfortunately.

Indeed. Was that the only reason that he wanted you to see the site? To know why he would be away? Before, you said he wanted you to see what it was like—what were your words?

My father wanted me to see the actual test site because he didn't think that words or pictures could describe it. He also wanted me to see the destruction, fortunately without Hiroshima bodies. The desert brush that we are looking at now was falling over sideways by the wind of the blast waves from the bomb and then the tremendous heat, fireball, and the infrared radiation which charred all the bushes and trees in place.

As we approached this area, all the bushes leaned out in a radial direction from the Ground Zero point. They were charred in place and they looked like something out of Transylvania. That was scary, that was really scary stuff.

～

The conversation faltered amid the desolation, each of us lost in our own thoughts, feelings, and memories.

My mind raced into the arid inner valleys of pain and accomplishment that were ultimately part of that grand test, which in time would engulf Oppenheimer, my father, Dana's father, and so many others in the shadow it cast on the world. From that moment in 1945, through the Cold War, into the 21st century, the fear lives behind the conscious daily life of most of the world as it stretches into the future.

Oppenheimer knew its consequences immediately— at the moment of the explosion he uttered the line from the Bhagavad Gita, "I have become Shiva, the destroyer of worlds." Not too long after that famous quote he would say, "We are all bastards."

I felt like I was in a slow-moving toy car with no real control over the wheel or accelerator, pretending that I was driving my tiny car down this road that Dana once traveled with his father.

～

Vee, my wife, was just asking how I felt traveling through here so many years later. There's a problem because I've been to White Sands a number of times as an adult in the process of launching sounding rockets for x-ray astrophysics experiments. That kind of [overlies] the other experience. So a lot of what I see now reminds me more of those rocket launches. When we get to the actual bombsite, my feelings may change. Right now, I am calmly interested in what we're seeing with a variety of strange-looking bunkers and towers. There was a sign a few minutes ago. There's another bunker coming up, "Missile Impact Area." We've gone by two huge bunkers and there are two more bunkers here on the side.

Is that where they store, or used to store, missiles?

No, I think those are instrumentation centers.

[*After forty-five minutes on a long, winding, two-lane road through desert sand, rocks, and military warning signs, we arrived at Trinity where, sixty-three years earlier, one age ended and another began.*]

At the entrance to the chain-link fence was what looked like a huge, sawed-out bunker.

What's that?

That's Jumbo. It was a containment bomb bottle; there isn't much left of it now. The top and bottom of it have been cut away. The idea was, since the first implosion bomb was plutonium, and plutonium was extremely scarce, they built a heavy steel bottle to contain the explosion. If it turned out to be a good bomb, then it would vaporize in steel. If it turned out to be a fissile, which is what they were afraid of, the implosion process might not bring all the plutonium together properly. If that was the case, then they hoped to be able to recover the plutonium. That was the idea of putting it in the bottle. But they gained more confidence about the implosion process as time went on, so they never used Jumbo.[46]

How come there is just part of it left?

I don't know, I guess they just decided to cut it in pieces.

What else do you remember seeing?

Until we got down into the actual depression, where the sand had been melted into green glass and re-deposited, it was a crunchy layer of trinitite that we walked on when we got to the site.

[*The pamphlet at the site states that at Ground Zero, trinitite can still be found in the area. It warns that it is still radioactive and must not be picked up.*]

Pamphlet from the Trinity Site

I'll describe walking into Ground Zero from the fence when I saw it as a kid. We arrived in an army car with Lieutenant Howard Bush driving. He was the head of the Army detachment at the test site. We approached a nice paved asphalt road. The road we are driving along now was in perfect shape all the way down to Ground Zero. It seemed to go for a very long way. I asked my father about it, and he explained that the surface of the road was vaporized and melted—that after the bomb a huge cloud developed and dissipated. It then gradually cooled to a very smooth surface, a perfect road.

Ground Zero was so deep I couldn't see over the rim. Of course I was only twelve. It was like a dish or a saucer. It didn't look like a crater, which is how I thought it would look. I was surprised—like a giant hand punched the ground down.

~

On this day a half-century later a beautiful monarch butterfly with perfectly symmetrical orange, black, and white designs on its wings circled Ground Zero. The site just looked like a fence around a big circle—a gigantic zero etched on this patch of desert. The monument—a pyramidal obelisk—was in the center of a big grassy field. A monument of Fat Man stood off to one side of the obelisk. There were more butterflies, crickets jumping in the grass, yellow daisies, and red stinging fire ants that sometimes feed on the crickets and can kill small animals. The red ants were ominous; they made me nervous.

I walked around the perimeter where time-lapse photos documented the four seconds it took for the explosion to form into the shape of a mushroom cloud. I don't think that people come here as if it is a typical tourist attraction, and yet they stand by the obelisk—which looks like a single tombstone of the birth of the Atomic Age—smile, and have their pictures taken.

⌇

One of the things that strikes me is the beautiful mountains and prairie, the innocence of it all. It looks like a lovely place—nice blue sky and sunshine, a light breeze; it's a comfortable temperature. That's pretty much the way it was for three years when I was a kid in Los Alamos. I really appreciated the weather and mountains of New Mexico. At that time, I had no idea, of course, that they were building an atomic bomb.

Later on, after my father could talk about it, one of the things he told me was that [military] intelligence obtained blueprints of the first Nazi B2 Horton, basically the first stealth bomber. It could fuel a rocket. The top scientists at Los Alamos laid out the blueprints on a table. At that point they were sure that Hitler had gotten the bomb and the main reason they were racing like crazy was to harness fission to make the bomb—to show it could be done. The first country that did it was going to win the war flat out.

My father said that when they laid those prints out, it was chilling. They surmised the only reason for going to all that trouble to make rockets was to carry a nuclear payload. They were so afraid that they sent radiology teams to Great Britain with different types of radiation-measuring instruments. So they surmised that when the first nuclear blast would go off in London they could help the British delineate where you could be safely inside or outside the city. They assumed the bomb would first be dropped on England. They were quite petrified of this possibility, and I think that was the main motivation to finish the bomb as soon as possible.

That must have been extremely frightening. How do you feel, being here now?

I feel disconnected from the reality I described to you earlier. In the sense that it's a nice day; there is a nice breeze blowing. I actually found it more chilling when we were in the National Atomic Museum in Albuquerque [now the National Museum of Nuclear Science and History] where I was standing by the casings of one of the bombs that fell accidentally off the coast of Spain. It was a hydrogen bomb, and the casing was quite authentic. As a matter of fact, if you look around at the back of it, there is a Department-of-Defense imprint. It's the real thing. It isn't very big—about a foot-and-a-half or two in diameter, six-to seven-foot-long—and it could wipe out a whole city. Now that was scary.[47]

The replica of Fat Man on the truck at Ground Zero here at Trinity near the obelisk is more impressive from where we are, about a thousand yards away. It affects me even today. I can see the mountain ranges on the brightest of days lighting the surrounding area for miles. Everyone was absolutely delighted and, at the same time, somewhat terrified. It was exactly my father's reaction. I think it was almost everybody's reaction who witnessed it. You can read all sorts of books about how people felt about it. Beyond that, I sure wish mankind lots of luck. [We both laugh nervously.]

Do you ever think about the radiation you might have been exposed to when you were just twelve? After all, it was just weeks after the test. Did you have fear about that during subsequent years?

I had a lot of faith in my father's judgment about that. I'm also surprised I'm still alive.

❦

We spent another hour at the site. Dana told some of his story standing at the obelisk while people gathered with great interest, listened, and asked questions. I walked the perimeter and inward to Ground Zero twice.

As we drove northwest out of the military base to Interstate 380, this time without an escort, I glanced back at the empty spot that from 1942 until now has defined a way of thinking and living in the world, a world where there are as many forms of fear and security in the guise of war and peace as there are Shiva's many arms.

We drove through Socorro County down I380 and soon arrived at the small town of San Antonio just before the intersection with I25. Between Pino and Miera Streets—at 79 Main Street—is the Owl Café and Bar. The Owl is famous for its green—chili cheeseburgers, but also because it is the original "Atomic Café" where Oppenheimer, Hans Bethe, Teller, and many other scientists on their way to and from Trinity would stop, rest, and discuss the fate of science and the world over cheeseburgers. Dana was disappointed it was not open. Being a vegetarian, I was not too disappointed.

❦

Dana died four years after our journey to Ground Zero from a heart condition at the age of sixty-eight. I was shocked and saddened when I called and Vee told me. I am so grateful he decided to travel with me on this, our shared pilgrimage into the past.

PART IV

My (Extended) Nuclear Family

Chapter 20

My Siblings (David and Sheri)

David Steinberg

In the spring of 2004 just outside of Fiddletown,
California in Amador County—up a long, winding private
road, across a stream, and past the vineyard to the top of
a hill in the Sierra foothills—I sit with my brother in his
living room. I ask him to speak into my tiny tape recorder.
David, two-and-a-half years older than me, three years
younger than my sister Sheri, is certainly not one with
unformed opinions but is, nevertheless, not thrilled at the
prospect of talking in general. His wife, Tracy, urges him
on and, after a brief glance out the window to the brown
hills and his two llamas, Mannix and Quolque, in the field
below, I ask for his thoughts concerning Dad's role in the
Manhattan Project.

There wasn't much about the Manhattan Project that had any
influence on me except, indirectly, my interest in science.
Historically I was very interested in the Project and also in
that part of the Second World War, but this interest was not
significantly different than my interest in other historical
topics such as ancient Egypt or, say, Alexander the Great.

There wasn't any direct influence of the Project in either my approach to science or in any other aspect of my life.

What I remember of talking to our father about the Project is that he held the same views as nearly everyone else at that time: that it was essential for the United States to get the bomb prior to Germany. There were rumors that Germany was beyond the United States in their production schedule and a belief that the German scientists were as capable as those in the United States of having a Manhattan-type project. They felt it was essential to defeat Germany, or at least to have the bomb before Germany did. When the War in Europe ended on May 8, 1945, and the testing at White Sands succeeded on July 15, many scientists, including our father, had second thoughts about using the A-bomb against the Japanese.

The scientists' influence on that decision was completely discounted. The decision was completely political—and the argument for it was that they estimated a million casualties with the invasion of the Japanese home islands and that it would be advantageous to end the war quickly. An additional consideration at the Yalta Conference of 1945 was that Stalin was redirecting his interest toward the Pacific, and Truman wanted to ensure that the war ended before Russia was involved in the Pacific.

Science had a profound influence in my life, but not particularly the Manhattan Project other than as a historical entity. It didn't influence my views of nuclear energy or any of the other political aspects of the sixties. My views come from a relatively substantial scientific background, which allows me to evaluate the various aspects of nuclear issues. [David has a Bachelor of Science in biology and mathematics from Stanford and completed course work for Ph.D.s in metamathematics and theoretical physics at the University of California Berkeley and Davis. He also has an M.D. from UC Davis and is a radiologist.]

Can you expand on why you think that most scientific people have similar opinions about the issue?

Understanding the science involved and the realization that, at the time, there was no real need to extend beyond what they already had. Unfortunately, because of the basic characteristics of humanity, there was no chance that, once the genie was out of the bottle, it was ever going to get put back in. It was, in many respects, a foregone conclusion that if there were improvements that could be made they would be made—in spite of the arguments of a lot of the prominent people in the Project. But those were political situations and, though it probably would have been better if they had not been taken or if there had been some other political alternatives that would have minimized the arms race that followed, in living through it, it just seemed like that was the way things were. It was just what was happening when I was growing up.

What are your views on nuclear energy?

We probably would have been a lot better off if we had worked more on that technology. Fission energy is cleaner fuel, and if they had resolved a lot of the issues prior to trying to implement the technology, there wouldn't have been a lot of the problems that still exist. Realistically speaking, from a political standpoint, fission energy is not going to happen because of the public response. Fusion energy would be great, but that's also a little bit further off, and it's unclear if the general public hysteria about nuclear energy would extend to fusion energy. In terms of the disposal of waste, which turned out to be one of problems of fission energy, fusion energy would obviously not have that problem, and the fuel is a lot more prevalent. So that would be a good choice if they could ever get it to work. Now, whether the public would ever endorse the use of fusion is another question.

What are your views on the future of the world and how nuclear weapons would progress or regress in the future? If you could look into the world fifty to one-hundred years from now, what do you think you would see?

In terms of nuclear weapons, it will probably stabilize the way things are, with the major superpowers minimizing the number of weapons that they have. I'm not optimistic about the future of the human race, but not certain that the way we will manage to destroy ourselves will be with nuclear weapons. There's an infinite number of ways, and I'm sure we will come up with something that is probably biological that is more likely to get more out of control than nuclear weapons. I think we've surpassed the infancy of nuclear weapons without further disasters—though the Cuban missile crisis was close—but once you get through the infancy and through the adolescence and into maturity, chances are that that's the way we will destroy ourselves are diminished substantially.

How do you envision what people will think in the future about the development of the bomb?

It's already reached the historical realm. It was a response to the situation in Germany. It was one of the most amazing collections of scientific talent there has ever been [amassed] toward a particular project and it was an amazing technological and scientific and intellectual accomplishment. I don't think that anybody could argue that the motivation for it wasn't justified and understandable. The only part of it that is problematic is the eventual use when Germany was already defeated at the end; and that is argued in the political realm because it was a political decision and not a scientific one. It certainly brought together the top scientific minds in the world at the time, and it was an amazing intellectual accomplishment.

How do you see the fact that many of the top people who worked in the project were Jewish affecting what happened?

Many of the top scientists were Jewish and refugees from Europe, which obviously increased their motivation.

Chapter 21

My Siblings (David and Sheri)

Sheri Steinberg

In the blazing heat of the Sacramento Valley lies Davis, home to a campus of the University of California. It is as unmarked by hills and just as hot in the summer as the Chicago suburb where my sister Sheri, my brother David, and I grew up. Six years older than me, Sheri is a petite woman with very short hair which, when she was younger, hung from a ponytail on top of her head all the way down to her waist. It is white now and she has hazel eyes like my father's. When my father died, she thought to donate his eyes with their perfect eyesight so that someone else might see with 20/20 vision.

Sheri and I sat down in her air-conditioned home to talk. She served me iced tea and we began.

What comes to mind in regard to Dad's work on the project?

There were a lot of dimensions to it. There was the sense that he was involved in something important and that that was also expected of us. It was highly visible scientific research, even though it was top secret. And, although it was primarily research, there also was the responsibility for what it led to. There was an equal sense of pride and shame involved in the Manhattan Project.

Did he ever talk to you about it? I don't remember him saying anything to me.

No, never. I don't remember when I learned about the bomb itself. Even though we were living within walking distance of Stagg Field at the University of Chicago [site of the first underground atomic test] when I was young, none of it registered. We moved to Park Forest when I was five. The only time I ever heard him talk about science was when he came to my junior high science and high school biology classes. I only remember him conveying what I wasn't doing properly. I had this sense that there was an expectation of my going into science—and I was interested in science, either because of that expectation or on my own. I followed the expected path. After my junior year of high school, I went to Purdue for a summer science program. Then, after my senior year, I worked in the cancer research laboratory at the University of Chicago. Like most other things, though, it [the plan] was never stated. Going to Rice University was part of the plan, too, but it wasn't part of the plan for me to come home during my first year a week before Thanksgiving. But that's the way it worked out. I gave up a full four-year scholarship, too.

I didn't realize you had a full scholarship.

Four full years—room and board, books, everything paid. I was trying to stick with the program and thought that if I was involved in something Dad was interested in, it would be a way of getting his approval. I liked science anyway and enjoyed doing research. I soon went the other way, though. I wanted to get as far away as possible from it.

Why was that?

I wanted to follow my own path, not one that had been chosen for me. Breaking away was difficult, though, because things were never stated. You could never say, "I don't want to be a scientist" or "You can't push me to be a scientist," because I wasn't pushed—at least not overtly. So either way— coming or going—I ran into a brick wall. When I met Chuck, I defected to the humanities. I took science courses in college, but pretty much stayed in the arts and literature. Part of the reason I studied psycholinguistics in graduate school was that I saw it as a way of getting back to a middle ground— studying language from a scientific point of view. I dropped out of that too, though that's another story.

A number of years ago I typed Dad's name in an Internet search and found the petition that I never knew he had signed against the bombing, the one that was signed by scientists at the Met Lab and sent to Truman.

I wrote and edited a piece on that.

Really?! That petition changed my perception on how he felt about dropping the bomb.

He also went to the Atoms for Peace conference in Geneva.[48]

I don't remember that, although I do remember him going to meetings in Switzerland. Did you ever think about Dad's emotional state, the way he treated us? I've thought about it in terms of it coming from the incredible pressure for accomplishment he put on himself and then on us.

I didn't really think of him as having much of an emotional state other than anger and impatience. I think he was an unhappy man. One time, in the late eighties, we had a huge blowout and he broke down and cried. He said all he ever wanted to do was be a pro tennis player. Uncle Nate and Uncle Hank said, "Over our dead bodies," and made Dad go to college. [From the time he was fourteen, when both his parents died, he was raised by his brothers Nate, who was twenty-seven years older, and Hank, nineteen years older.] The only other times I'd ever seen him cry were when Pogo [our dog] and Uncle Hank died.

I believe he felt his brothers had commandeered his life; he was pretty much channeled into what they thought he wanted to do. He wasn't in touch with his feelings, although he enjoyed his career and was very good at it. He committed himself to the work, but I think the ambivalence he had went deeper. Working for a project that was opening up a whole new world of knowledge about the universe—but at the same time giving people the means to exterminate ourselves—fit right in to the kind of ambivalence he had about his not really doing what he wanted to do. But he never talked about it.

That's strange, because David [our brother] told me one time that he wanted to be a pro tennis player—he and Dad were both excellent tennis players—but told me not to tell Dad. So it was both of their secret ambitions.

He was obviously an athlete, though.

Tennis, golf, bowling—he excelled at all of them. He and his brothers were all athletes and Uncle Nate was a great swimmer; he almost competed in the Olympics.

When [Eugene] McCarthy was running for President in 1968 and I wanted Dad to put a bumper sticker on the car and he said, "No, you can't do that, you don't put things on the car." He was very adamant. I couldn't understand

*why a bumper sticker was such a big deal. I understand
it more now; the FBI had investigated him and other people he knew. People I've talked to said their parents were
watched even into the sixties. I found a letter he had written
for somebody saying that the other person had never been
a member of the Communist Party. Maybe there was also
some futility about trying to influence politics. The scientists were acutely aware of what the FBI was doing and the
surveillance and the problems they caused Oppenheimer as
well.*

People who do undercover or top-secret work are
under extraordinary stress. People who are basically inward,
who don't expose themselves in some ways, are suited for
that— despite the stresses. It's interesting that you mention
the politics and paranoia, because I tended to see it more as
a personality characteristic of his, as opposed to a political
necessity. He wasn't inclined to talk in the first place, but this
sanctioned it. It does create a certain paranoia and secrecy;
it sets up a wall between him and other people. Anyway, telling me about the tennis pro thing was the only time I saw him
real, showing his true feelings ...well, that and one other time
in Geneva with the watch when I ran away. [Our father had
bought watches for my mother and sister when we were in
Switzerland.] He was so young then, only thirty-seven.

What happened?

I was a pain in the neck on that trip. We went to Paestum
[in southern Italy, south of Naples] because I'd been studying Rome in school and wanted to see the ruins there. We'd
been driving around in the car cooped up for weeks. I was
acting up, saying I wouldn't do this and I wouldn't do that.
Dad said, "If you don't settle down and fly right you can't have

the watch. I'm going to take the watch back." I said, "I don't care. I don't want your stupid old watch anyway." We were in Renaissance Park in Geneva, and I took the watch off, threw it down, and ran.

Oh God, Mom must have had a fit.

Nobody ever talked about it after that, but he really lost it. I was just pushing and pushing—it was a battle of wills. I thought then that I wanted to win, but when I did and made him cry, I realized that's not what I wanted at all.

I felt the only time I had an emotional connection with him was when we were yelling at each other. When you were already in college, we had some terrible arguments.

Growing up I always felt the presence of the bomb without it being talked about, and yet I knew and wondered how he could have done that work. It is strange because I was born seven years after the end of the war.

I never felt that.

In a scene at the San Francisco Opera production of Doctor Atomic, Kitty Oppenheimer was rocking her baby as the scientists built the bomb on the other side of the stage. They lifted up the bomb and it was hanging over the crib for a good part of the second act. I turned to my friend and said, "That was me."

All I felt was the notoriety of it and the fact that he did something that affected the world. I did a project on the making of the bomb, a little companion book I wrote. [*A Historical Reader: The Atomic Bomb*, Houghton Mifflin, 2000] If anything, I subconsciously thought that if I could make myself as small as possible, maybe then he'd like me; this unfortunately manifested, for a time, in anorexia. There was that aspect of his work, but it didn't have to do with the bomb. It was the focus on the nuclear, minute parts of things that affected me.

That's interesting, because I used to feel like a ghost, like the atom was split inside me—that I could never be whole; that I was invisible.

Well, you were; that's why. I think he tended to see everything—especially his family—as a projection of him.

I felt overwhelmed by it all, which made me want to escape even more. Getting high and sixties music both helped and made it worse. The music and lyrics had always given me a place of connection and understanding, but getting high had led, at times, to a further dissociation from reality. Maybe it all affected me more profoundly; in high school I would come home every night and watch the numbers on the news of the dead in the Vietnam War. I connected all these wars together—the dropping of the atomic bomb in World War II, the Holocaust in Germany, and Vietnam.

Well, that's true. We grew up in different time periods. The Korean War was going on when I was young. I was born after World War II and, after Vietnam, I was grown and out of the house. I grew up during the Eisenhower boom. Even though we were only six years apart, it was a completely different era. The optimism and positivity and pulling together after the war was alive in the country. Then came the anti-communist scare and the McCarthy Era.

I'm sure that made Dad want to continue his closed-mouth policy on anything political.

[Mom and Dad went to Florida for a month every to escape the Chicago winters after they retired. One time after Dad died, I went down there, and Mom and I visited the

Holocaust Memorial in Miami.

Isn't that where the picture I have of yours was taken? [It shows a sculpture of one muscular arm and hand reaching up to the sky; at its base and climbing up its arm are life-size emaciated Holocaust survivors.]

Yes. Mom just wanted to get out of there, and I said, "Well I want to see the place first." She rushed through it like she was running from a tornado. On the way back to the apartment where she was staying she told me there was a cousin of hers who died in the Holocaust—shot and pushed into an unmarked grave. I never knew about it.

Really? I didn't know that either.

That was the only time she mentioned anything about the Holocaust and, somehow, growing up I just felt there were all these clouds of tragedies hanging over the house. So here was another example of keeping a secret. Not only did I already feel invisible, I wanted to disappear from everything I saw around me.

Changing focus—do you think that Dad's working on the Project had any effect on your spiritual or religious views?

No, I never really had a sense of what his spiritual views were. My sense of our religious upbringing was that it was very pro forma. I never sensed any commitment to core spiritual values. It was mostly learning Hebrew and following the ritualistic patterns. In terms of other values, one effect he had on me was that I developed a disdain for business. It seemed like there was something superior about going to a scientific laboratory every day rather than going into an office carrying a briefcase. Incorporating that value that we saw daily was powerful. I looked down for many, many years on people who were in business.

I felt that too—well, I still do to some degree. What are your views on nuclear energy and nuclear power plants?

Nuclear energy is always an energy that can be tapped but needs to be treated with a great deal of respect and not used lightly. The process requires extreme caution, and it's not a panacea. Fossil fuels are gone. We have to use other sources; we have to use what we have—solar, wind, water, and anything else we can find, even garbage.

How do you see the aftereffects of the bomb in terms of the world today?

I think everybody should trash their nuclear weapons. Just because you can do something doesn't mean that you should. I think that people need to turn their eyes inward and focus on solving the problems that we have as a race. The more lethal means we have at our disposal, the more likely we are to use them. Just like in Virginia [referring to the Virginia Tech killings]—guns do kill people if people have them, and so do nuclear weapons if we have them.

You spent a year in Japan teaching English. Did you go to Hiroshima?

I didn't get a chance to go. I thought about the fact that, indirectly, I was involved in the production of the bomb. Writing that book, I realized that the decision to use the bomb was not one that was taken lightly. I think Truman was in a terrible position.

When he was vice-president he didn't even know about the Manhattan Project.

I know; he was thrust into it all. But he put together the

people and acted as responsibly as anyone could under the circumstances. They really thought using the bomb would be saving lives. The thing is, though, how do you ever make that up to anybody, to a people, or a nation? It becomes a racial stain the way our treatment of African-Americans is. I did think about it, living among the Japanese and feeling their disdain and distancing, though it had nothing to do with the bomb.

There was no way they could have known that you were the daughter of a scientist who worked on the A-bomb.

Exactly. They didn't know; they just hated every gaijin [foreigner]. It's hard being treated that way. I was working eleven to twelve hours a day, coming home, and trying to study Japanese. I'd try to speak to people and they'd just walk right by me. Of course the generation I was dealing with was far removed from World War II. Most of them weren't alive, because if they'd been there at the time the bombs were dropped, they most likely wouldn't be around now. I'm really sorry I didn't go to Hiroshima; I did feel something of a compulsion to go there and somehow make amends.

Does anything else come to mind concerning the topic in relationship to you personally or globally?

I would have just as soon have not had the involvement, even though it had a minimal impact on me. I think there was a sense of being faced with the consequences of your actions. There was a sense that not knowing is not an excuse. I don't know if that comes from being personally involved in it—because I learned about it like everyone else would learn about it, as history. My learning about it was not done in a family environment. In that sense I don't see myself as being that different from anybody else who would look at the situation and try to figure out what lessons to take from it. It's interesting that you feel that personal sense of involvement, because I never really did.

I know, I still can't explain why.

Chapter 22

My Cousins (Abigail, Jesse, and Daniel)

Abigail Abraham

My cousin Abigail Abraham, the youngest in the family, lives in suburban Washington, DC. Her father, my mother's brother, had worked with my father at the University of Chicago Met Lab, but most of his work was on the hydrogen bomb. She is five years my junior, and we grew up close to each other in the Chicago suburbs. We talked on the phone one day in July of 2008.

I began by asking Abigail if her father had talked to her much about his work with the Manhattan Project.

Very little. He talked more about the hydrogen work and the gas diffusion work he was doing at the university than the atom bomb. It might have had something to do with the time frame and of secrecy requirements and clearances.

I didn't know he worked on the hydrogen bomb until I talked with Daniel.

He had a patent on one of the processes for tritium for the hydrogen bomb [Tritium production by neutron-irradiation of aluminum-lithium alloys (U.S. Patent No. 3100184,

1963).][49]

I didn't know that they were working on the H-bomb in Chicago. I thought that was all done in Los Alamos.

He went to Los Alamos a couple times, but I believe that some of the work that he did on that was in Chicago as well. I don't know how many times he went out to Los Alamos, though. That was in the fifties [March 1, 1954] when the hydrogen bomb was tested.

Was that the test over the Bikini Atoll?

Yes. He wasn't allowed to go there and watch the test. It was some political decision that I don't remember. Daniel probably will; Mom almost certainly will.

Do you think, in the little bit that your father said, he was for the bomb being dropped?

You mean did he believe that it was the right decision? Yes, I believe so.

Did you get a sense when you were growing up about how he related to his work on the bomb?

I knew that he did war work and that he wouldn't talk about most of it. I remember when I was in high school asking him what specifically he was working on at that time. I knew he was a research scientist, chemical physicist, and at the time I asked him he said that he was measuring the viscosity of liquid helium-3. My understanding from occasional discussions was that part of the reason he got into the low-temperature work was that it was a byproduct of some of the war work that he did. Not only was his interest piqued, but certain war work produced byproducts that he could work on.

Part of the effect of the secrecy can be seen in the scientific journals. There was, in a brief time period, a massive reduction in publications by all the top scientists who were then working on the Manhattan Project. Everything that they were doing became classified. You could look at the journals and see they went from being a certain number of pages to being half or a third of the size they were. Someone could see all the names that were not there anymore and figure out that something was going on by what was not being published.

It would be very interesting to see what sorts of assumptions and inferences could have been made—and the extent to which Dad had been publishing and then all of sudden he wasn't. Neither was your dad and neither were any of the other people.

Was he part of the hydrogen-bomb project for quite a while?

Sure, he should have been out at the test. And when was the test, 1956?

Yes.

He was doing work like that for some period of time.

I have discovered that, for my sister and brother, the bomb didn't have much of a personal impact; but, for me, it always seemed to be there. I don't know if I was just picking up that my dad had this conflict with it and his conflict brought me to that place as well. Part of it could have been the rebellion in the sixties and seventies against nuclear power.

I remember hearing about protests pertaining to the bomb being dropped—that it was a terrible thing. People in school may have known that my dad worked on the bomb, or I may have mentioned it. I remember there was debate but I don't remember that I had personal issues as a result or that I had anything to resolve.

It was a terrible outcome with what we would now call collateral damage. However, the more I've read the more I believe it saved a lot of lives—certainly ours and probably Japanese lives as well.

Well, collateral damage is one way to describe it, I guess.

It probably saved many American lives, which would have been military more than not. But any country wants to save its own people's lives irrespective of whether they are military or civilian.

In a certain context, given how we deal with collateral damage and our differences, I feel—and this is going very far afield—that the "political" way in which America is now waging war is not right. I think we fight wars politically now and not militarily and I believe that result is not good.

What is not good?

Waging war the way we do in a political arena: it makes it nearly impossible to achieve the military objectives. Wars are always going to be somewhat political, but I think that the public relations for the wars that we have been in have been badly handled. If the government is going to choose to go to war, then the PR [Public Relations] should be handled better and decisions should be made on the basis of military need not on the basis of PR. But that is a separate issue.

Do you feel that having a father who had a role in working on the Manhattan Project and the key H-bomb had an effect on your course in life?

No. I think that his being a scientist had a substantial effect on my upbringing—the way in which I approach problems, the kind of household in which I grew up, the kind of person he was and, of course, the environment he created for us. I don't have any reason to believe that there was any particular uniqueness to it as a result of the Project that he worked on. I think that he was shaped by his era. He was an ungodly bright, analytical scientist. I don't know if there would have been much of a difference had he never worked on the H-bomb and only worked on poison gases or other kinds of war work, or possibly other kinds of scientific research and not war work. He might have talked more about the work that he had done, which, of course, he didn't do. I think it affected the household some that he didn't talk about some of his past work because he said it was classified, and we simply got used to not discussing anything that was classified.

Same with my dad.

Did Sheri or David think that the war work had any effect on their upbringing?

Not really.

I'm not surprised.

I'm not surprised with David. With Sheri I'm sort of surprised. Other people I have talked to said their dads talked about their work on the Manhattan Project with their families quite a bit when they were growing up. Both your father [my uncle] and my father never talked about it.

We would get stories about Los Alamos—not the work, but there might be pictures of a square dance they went to or a piece of Indian jewelry they brought home, or they would say they were camping out there—things like that. When they were in Los Alamos they acquired items that had a Southwestern feel to them. But none of this had to do with the substance of being on the Project.

He once mentioned—and I don't remember who this involved—that there was an explosion that went awry and one of the scientists decided he had to take certain action in order to stop a greater catastrophe, knowing that if he did that he was going to get killed as a result of the radiation or the effect of the bomb. If he had not taken action he probably would have been killed anyway, but so would other people. There were extremely rare occasions when a story like that would come up, but as far as the core work itself, no. That was not discussed. At least not that I remember.

It's interesting—maybe it's Daniel and me being the same age—I actually thought about this before I met Daniel [her brother] for the anti-nuclear march in New York in 1984.

What are your views on nuclear bombs and...

I hope we never detonate any.

I guess, to sum up, your dad didn't talk about it much, except for a few times in high school when it came up.

We may have had a discussion at some point about what he thought of dropping the bomb. I don't remember specifically and I certainly remember he was not opposed to it. And the specific war work he absolutely did not discuss. The peripheral matters yes, but not the specific work.

As a whole it doesn't really seem that you could say that it had much of an effect on you personally, in terms of how you look at things in the world or how you look at this issue or how you live your life really. Is this true?

I think that's true. It's not like I said, "Oh my god, Dad was part of this incredible bomb and it was a horrible thing, and as a result I'm inherently opposed to any kind of nuclear devices or nuclear testing or nuclear power or anything else, ever." No, that is not the result it had. It sounds like there was more of an effect on you in that regard.

Yes, there was. I don't know what the roots are. In my talk with Sheri I know some of it was sandwiched into the Vietnam War having such a major effect on me, and war in general. I linked that up to the feeling of how could my father have worked on such a project with outcomes that were so horrible, and the irony of the original development and building of the bomb to fight Hitler—fighting one Holocaust by creating a different kind of holocaust.

That assumes that you think that the two of them are parallel, which I certainly don't. I'm not sure that I would use the term *holocaust*. I think I would reserve *holocaust* for something fairly specific. I generally don't think of working on the bomb as horrible. Technology often times is more value-neutral. I don't see that your dad or mine worked on something horrible. It's possible that you argue that the use to which it was put was bad; but, to me, that is sort of like saying the Internet is inherently horrible or not because it was used for the following bad things or good things. There are very few technological innovations that, as a value judgment, you can say are inherently bad.

This is more of a teenager's view; I look at it differently now. I don't say that because he worked on the bomb it was a horrible thing at the time. I think the aftermath and how it threw everything into the Cold War and what we are still doing with this is pretty bad.

I don't know. I think that generally your political views and mine are fairly divergent.

That's true.

I question the assessment of cause and effect, because if this cause didn't happen, it doesn't necessarily mean that something else just as bad wouldn't have happened. Is the bomb the thing that caused the Cold War?

On some level the Cold War probably would have happened anyway. But at this point in time, how many nuclear weapons do we need? Now they are redoing the entire arsenal at Livermore Lab. It's as if the ones we have now are not going to be good enough.

Well, at some point the detonation process and the triggers go bad. Whether the warheads are bad—I don't know enough about it.

I don't know either; although if we are reducing the overall stockpile of bombs worldwide, why replace them?

I want the United States to be stronger than other countries. How that is accomplished and how we make choices is very difficult. How much of an arsenal we should have is a difficult choice. I don't know the answers to those things. I don't think there is negotiation with certain people. I think we have very divergent views on these types of issues.

That's very true, but I love you anyway.

Chapter 23

My Cousins (Abigail, Jesse, and Daniel)

Jesse Abraham

I called my cousin Jesse—Daniel's younger and Abigail's older brother–who lives in Washington, DC, with his wife Amy. One of their sons is now at the University of Chicago. After a few minutes of catching up, I told him about my project and asked if he would be willing to add his voice to the stories, impressions, and feelings I had been gathering of those who had grown up in families so close to the development of nuclear weapons.

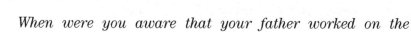

When were you aware that your father worked on the Manhattan Project and the H-bomb?

It was a long time before I was born that my father worked on the Project. I probably became more aware in my high school years about his involvement. Growing up I thought of my father as working with liquid helium. I would say, even to this day, that his engagement on any of the atomic-bomb research, as opposed to the hydrogen bomb, really was minimal. I thought of his efforts during the war on poison gas when he was up at Northwestern University. The connection with the hydrogen bomb would have been in the early 1950s. There was a gap when I hadn't thought much about what he was doing between 1942 and 1944.

My parents went to Los Alamos in 1950, which was in relation to the H-bomb work. I don't believe he was there before then, which means he would have been part of the group working at the University of Chicago. He had several patents of processes that went into the hydrogen bomb. He made an independent contribution—it wasn't just that he was a worker bee, but he actually contributed ideas. I always thought that was closer to his achievements than the atomic bomb.

Yes, Daniel mentioned the patent he had for the tritium process.

He wasn't particularly boastful, but I wouldn't call my father a shy man.

A bit of an understatement, I'd say. [Both of us laugh.]

Yes, I'd agree.

At that time you didn't talk about things; but other than his aura of self-importance and cleverness, he didn't substantiate that with stories of importance. I think when he ran for school board he mentioned his work on the hydrogen bomb and wrote about his work in journals.

Do you remember what he said about the hydrogen bomb?

There were a couple of family stories which, if you ask my brother, you discover one story when he made a presentation and it was not well received. But Teller was in the room and supported "Abraham's idea," so he received support from The Great One. However, I don't think my father thought well of him. My father antagonized the wrong people, so that in the end he was disinvited to go watch the Eniwetok hydrogen bomb test.

Daniel talked about that; probably a very good thing.

He used the Abraham tact; his personality—that was just the way it was.

That is completely true! Did he ever talk about how he felt about his work? And how do you feel about his involvement?

I didn't sense any regret, disappointment, or shame, or any emotions that one might feel if one had contributed to something and then in the end found that it was not good for mankind. He was a thoughtful man and somewhat self-reflecting, but I don't recall, at any point, that he felt it was inappropriate [to do] that work. Though he didn't boast much, I think he felt pride in his accomplishments and the recognition that came with that, independent of the bomb's ultimate possible use. As a scientist it is more like, I cracked the problem that was put in front of me; I solved it, and that helped further the goals of the organization I was working for.

Growing up, we—Daniel, Abigail, and I—were bred with a pride in his accomplishments and bred to be impressed with his many qualities. As we became teenagers and young adults we became in some ways slightly less impressed with him, but with the distance of age we can appreciate some of his stronger points.

One of the other family stories was about my mother coming home from work and somebody at the house picking pieces of glass out of his face.

Yes, Daniel told that story—something about, Don't

worry, Mrs. Abraham, the glass was sterile.

What he was doing was hardly risk free.

That's for sure.

With all the talk of the best [greatest] generation, while my father was not fighting overseas on D-Day, he did his part. I don't feel any shame or disappointment that the Abraham family heritage did not contribute to the United States in its time of need.

I read a book on Oppenheimer and the war and appreciate the science and organization that was necessary to bring off what was a substantial scientific and operational accomplishment. The world is a dangerous place and, while it's true that the United States government is not benign—certainly not what it represents itself to be— many people in the White House at that time, I like to think, were not as disappointing as the current occupants. During that time there was some reasonable and moral purpose in the world to maintain safety, so I don't doubt that was an appropriate effort for the United States to undergo.

You're speaking of the hydrogen bomb?

Yes. I don't have any moral reservations about his work and don't feel any disappointment about his behavior or any personal responsibility for feeling that I was supported by money that was paid to him for work that he did. Some people look back and feel shame that their ancestors had slaves and say, that is how I got to where I am today. Some people might challenge that, and I'm saying I don't feel a shred of that relative to my father's work on something that is a weapon to kill people.

I was surprised to find out that your dad had worked on

the H-bomb. My feeling is that there was already a weapon that was more powerful than anything needed to be. Why make something so much more powerful than the atomic bomb? When you eventually have to negotiate with people, you actually have to live in the world with these people. And a weapon like that just contributes to the danger and the horrific consequences of what could ultimately happen.

That's right, and it makes the cost of it and the error in judgment that much greater. Unfortunately, I have not studied the period to understand all the motivations. I was underwhelmed with Ronald Reagan's characterization of the Soviet Union as an evil empire when he made that statement back in the early eighties. I certainly have come to think that the Soviet Union was a terrible place, and now it is probably not much better. I can understand, when engaged with that type of foe, that you might say, My responsibility is to be stronger than them—and certainly for them to believe and for us to believe that we are no weaker than them.

But their economy was diminished and weak. When it finally came down to it, wouldn't they realize how poor and how badly off the people in Russia were?

The people being impoverished does not mean that the government was not dangerous.

That's true.

When I think about the H-bomb or this sort of issue, if anything, it's probably pride in that: when challenged, my father made a substantive and intellectual contribution. Myself, not being a scientist but a social scientist, I appreciate the dynamic of research and trying to push the field and come up with ideas that are different than anyone's had before. Did it make an impact? He delivered at an important time and I have respect for his accomplishment.

Have you ever been to Los Alamos?

My wife, Amy, and my two boys, David and Jeremy, went as tourists to Los Alamos back in March. We went to the museum and tried to find names of people to recognize in documents there. I felt a familial affinity connected to that time, although I saw no mention of any family member. There were some pictures of some professors I had in college from thirty to forty years earlier.

Did you take a tour of Los Alamos?

We went to two museums: first, the historical museum, which had a lot of pictures and descriptions about what life was like living in Los Alamos during the war. It showed how Groves developed the town as a restricted secret compound. We also went to the Bradbury Museum, which is run by the official Department of Energy. It documents the history of the bomb and its development and is less about the people and social dynamics. It didn't occur to me that there was a tour of the facility available.

I'm not sure if there is. [When I went a few years later I found that there is one, and received a personal tour from Dana Mitchell (See Chapter 19 Part 3).]

There were restricted areas; we were on the public highway and there was a guard at one end and a guard at the other end and there was a restricted space on the map. It showed it was a public highway and we went, Huh, what's going on here?

I've looked at the map; it is strange. I suppose no one goes up that way unless they are going to Los Alamos.

What are your views on nuclear power and nuclear weapons these days?

It's hard to be for them. There is a resurgence in support for nuclear energy, given that there are two things that have changed: the price of oil has gone up and the concern about greenhouse gases. I don't know if it's really true that nuclear might be cleaner and have less effect on the atmosphere. Of course, there are all the concerns that we still haven't figured out—like how to store this stuff— and it just seems bizarre that's completely ignored in debates.

Livermore Lab received the contract over Los Alamos to redesign and build their whole pile of nuclear weapons. They are going to make the new generation of weapons.

The old ones are degrading—the uranium isn't in good shape or the casings are degrading.

So what are they going to do with all the old ones?

If it's true that the old ones are falling apart, I could understand that—it's necessary for the United States to have some nuclear weaponry. The world can't think that the United States doesn't have any when countries like Pakistan, France, Israel, or—heaven forbid—Iran would have a nuclear weapon; it would be just incredibly destabilizing.

Yes, but they could make fewer—or, better yet, stop making them.

Maybe, I don't know. The industrial complex is probably overdoing it because that is what they do.

Changing focus—Daniel remembered, as I did, standing on that scale and putting our hands in to see if the Geiger counter went off when you left the Lab.

I do remember that. I also remember being impressed

with how much mercury there was in beakers. I don't know if it was to measure temperature or what [Jesse's father Bernard worked in low-temperature chemistry]; it just seems like there were quarts of mercury, a fascinating substance. There were a lot of things around there that were very fascinating and very dangerous. It wasn't exactly a safe environment. I remember going to his lab and seeing all this big equipment and all the dials and wondering what it was all for.

Is there anything you would like to add?

As an adult I've mellowed on some of my father's personality characteristics that weren't so positive. I don't second-guess the need for the research he was engaged in or even the projects that he was on—the atomic bomb or even the hydrogen bomb. The atomic bomb was during a time of war and there was a race against time; and the scientists working on the other side were reportedly trying to do similar work. I don't feel any moral ambiguity about what was happening in the United States or those efforts or the extent that he contributed, which was admirable. I am proud of his contribution.

Chapter 24

My Cousins (Abigail, Jesse, and Daniel)

Daniel Abraham

*My cousin Daniel and I grew up along similar paths—
the same age, both with artistic pursuits. He is a professional cartoonist and I am a poet and photographer. Our
fathers worked on the Manhattan Project at the University
of Chicago, then at Argonne National Laboratory—a
lab that grew out of the Project. My father, Ellis, and
Daniel's father, Bernard (my mother's brother), met at the
University; Bernard introduced my father to my mother
after he saw a picture of her Bernard carried in his wallet.
Daniel and I grew up in the suburbs of Chicago (Oak Park
and Park Forest, respectively) and would see each other
four or five times a year on holidays and other family
occasions. No matter what the occasion, animated discussions of science moderated by my father and uncle would
be the centerpiece at the dinner table.*

*Daniel and I sat down for our phone interview
on a Sunday in the spring of 2007, each in our respec-
tive homes. I sat comfortably on the blue couch in my
two-story condo, twenty minutes north of Berkeley, tape
recorder connected into the phone cradle, tabby cat inquis-
itive but meowing for food. Daniel was in New York in*

*his Manhattan brownstone walk-up apartment, always
ready with intelligence, insight, and a plethora of words.
Memories spewed forth, stretching across our flyover
Midwest homes that held secrets of our childhoods and our
familial connection to the bomb.*

*I'm interested in memories you have from growing up in
relation to the bomb?*

I'm assuming that, like us, you used to go to the Lab as a
kid. I'm not sure what Uncle Ellis was working on when Dad
was working on low-temperature chemistry.

*High-energy physics. We'd go to see his lab and the
cyclotron when we'd go to Argonne.*

So tell me, did you get a kick, like we did, out of checking the radiation levels when you left the building, sticking
your hands in the slots, and waiting to see if the light turned
from green to red?

*Yes, it was exciting—our own private Science and
Industry Museum. It was fun until I was older and realized
the consequences of what we were doing.*

Seeing how radiated we might have become was a big
thrill. The tricks that Dad used to do at the Lab, not only for
us, but for classes that came on field trips, which had nothing
to do with nuclear things were also interesting and exciting,
such as freezing rubber into liquid nitrogen and breaking a
piece of flexible rubber tube on a counter. You remember that
stuff, right?

Not particularly those but I remember stories of

elements being bombarded, and later on, my father's excitement at working on moon rocks. I asked him if he could bring a rock home so I could see one. He said, "No, they aren't to leave the Lab."

It was all a big thrill. The Lab was just a mysterious place with a weird smell and quiet hums and weird-looking machinery. On occasion we'd go and look at the reactor; and I didn't know what we were supposed to see. You remember the reactor, don't you?

Of course. How could I forget?

There were a couple of times when field trips from the school would go to the Lab. This was, of course, the sixties, and science was king. The space program was just beginning, and going to see real live scientists was a huge thrill for kids in public elementary schools.

We never went there on a school trip, but you were closer to the Lab than we were. But boy, we got to see them every day!

In some sense, when people start talking about nukes and stuff like that, don't you feel like, "Well, yeah, but…"

I know exactly what you mean.

I won't say the atom is like your favorite stuffed animal and mine; but we grew up close to this, so it didn't seem strange or scary. It's not like the atom is your friend. It was just one of those things, a part of growing up. All the atomic power and everything that went along with it was just part of our lives.

Yes, exactly—the atom is our friend [said like a TV commercial].

There was a matter-of-fact attitude growing up that all of

this was part of our everyday world. We grew up in a family with a particularly favored group of people. During that time A-bombs were in the news quite often. They still had atmospheric and underground tests, and we were closer to that. There was this feeling that we were somehow organically connected to great events, even if we had no particular participation in them.

Yes, I still felt much closer to the core of that world—the wonder, the danger, and the tragedy of it all.

We grew up with a close personal nexus to a semi-secret government installation. Everyone knew it was there, but you couldn't get in without an ID and some sort of authorization to be there. You and I had a personal casualness to all of this bizarre equipment. I was a science idiot, and I presume that you weren't a particularly big science person either.

That's right. When I was young, my dad would bring me science kits. I'd mix chemicals together and make things and I'd try to understand what was behind it. But I could not grasp easily what I was seemingly supposed to understand. David and Sheri were much more inclined to grasp scientific and mathematical concepts.

I remember so clearly the anti-nuclear march in Manhattan in the eighties. We went back to your apartment, where you drew a cartoon with a fetus inside an atomic bomb, which you said you don't even remember doing. You said, "We could have had our own contingent at the march" and wrote "Children of the Manhattan Project." That is what actually gave me the idea for these interviews.

As I said, I've drawn thousands of cartoons and this was, what, fifteen to twenty years ago? It doesn't mean that it wasn't heartfelt. I think that I had a proprietary feeling about the whole nuclear thing. Don't you?

Yes, but as I mentioned, I still feel conflicted. When the anti-nuclear movement came along, I agreed with not developing more nuclear energy, but I still felt paralyzed and caught in the middle. As you said, though, we were still somehow organically connected to the atomic world and all the confusion it brought. I guess that's why I'm still looking for clarity and resolution.

Both of our fathers were favored by fortune, favored by heaven, to an astounding degree. They may have lived in the Golden Age, if you will, but we are the recipients of that as a Silver Age living among Bronze Age people. I'm absolutely serious about that. I think we have much to be thankful for as a result of this.

I remember seeing a mimeograph with an illustration of someone building a cinder-block wall and a baby cradled in one arm. It said: "The Family Fallout Shelter." This was lying around the house, probably from the late fifties. Dad never bought into that crap; he said if they hit us, a fallout shelter is not going to do a damn bit of good—so don't worry about it. There was sort of that hard edge to his attitude about it, like, there is hysteria in the world and this is what the situation is, so just don't worry about it. You assume that we know what is really going on, not in terms of what the government is doing, but in terms of knowing that if somebody nukes Chicago we're dead anyway. So who cares? In the meantime, you do what you do. You guys never built a fallout shelter, did you?

Absolutely not.

I can't imagine your father doing that.

Or your father. No, it was hard enough to get him to have the recreation room built—which, for thirty years, was called the "new room." Maybe it was named after New Chem! He didn't like mundane matters.

I remember seeing pictures when we would go to Argonne— pictures of the early days. There were a couple of times when the small reactors caught fire and blew up. There were pictures of these disasters that were posted on the walls back in the day, and the scientists who worked there were all very mellow about it.

I suppose they had to be; it was their daily world.

They worked with it as a matter of fact. Several of Dad's friends died from berylliosis poisoning from working in the machine shop and getting beryllium dust in their lungs because the safety levels were nowhere near what people demand today. When my mom and dad were first married, there was an explosion. If he had not received his safety goggles the day before, he would have been blinded.

Mom told the story: In the early days of their marriage, she came home and found him bandaged head to toe on the sofa, and his section head was there. The famous line was, "Don't worry, Mrs. Abraham, all the glass in him is sterile." He had been in an explosion; he had shards of glass in him, and they were all sterile. Not to worry.

Wow, of course, not to worry—typical. I never heard that story. How long did it take for him to recover from that?

I don't think too long. Several of his classmates were killed before he worked on the project—one of the poison-gas experiments that went awry—and I remember him saying in passing once, "I hate phosgene."[50]

I guess some of it got loose in the lab one day with a tragic outcome. It's one of the very vicious poison gases; it's worse than mustard gas. Mustard, chlorine and phosgene were all World War I gases. It burns more and it's more corrosive; it's a horrible thing. I think it's related to white phosphorus, which is also horrific.

People used to ask Dad if he felt bad about having worked on the bomb. His answer was always that he regretted that they did not get it done in time to drop it on Germany. It was a very sincere reply on his part. Your family was in Denmark—when was that?

In 1957 and 1958.

We were in England in 1960 and 1961. We did a lot of driving around the continent and we drove to Denmark, then through Germany. It was still only fifteen years after the war. Dad's German had a pronounced Yiddish accent. [laughter] The discomfort of being in Germany was quite immense.

We drove through Germany during our stay in Denmark in 1957 when we toured Europe. I think the goal was to get through there as fast as possible and get out.

My dad was doing low-level grunt work on the Project, and I'm assuming Ellis was, too, on the actual original atom bomb; because they were young—they were doctoral students—they were basically schlepping graphite blocks.

Well, I think they did a bit more than that. I found an article that my father wrote—it was published in the Journal of Chemical Education *in 1989, in it my Dad described how he was recruited to the Project. They did have quite a bit of responsibility, considering how young they were. They didn't talk about the particulars because the security was very high, especially after what happened to Oppenheimer.*

I was told by my dad, after they found out what they were actually working on and switched him over from the project on poison gas, that he came home sort of radiating [This pun, I assume, was intended.] excitement talking about a whole new source of power. That's all he could say to my mother, and even that was pushing it.

His really important work, was on the hydrogen bomb. The push to create the H-bomb was, of course, from Teller. They were trying to make the hydrogen bomb with deuterium—heavy water—and it wasn't working. They wanted to try tritium, but were having trouble producing it. Tritium doesn't occur naturally; it's an isotope of hydrogen. I'm not sure if they are neutrons or electrons. You can tell how good my science background is.[51]

Dad came up with a process for producing tritium and got the personal go-ahead from Teller. There was a secret meeting around 1950 at the Museum of Science and Industry in Chicago. He and Bernard Weinstock, his colleague at the time, developed the process and they went to Los Alamos to teach it to Teller's group. I'm told they made themselves quite obnoxious, basically young whippersnappers who were very full of themselves: "You couldn't figure out how to do this, and we did."

[In mock surprise]: Your father, obnoxious? I can't imagine that.

He had the arrogance of youth untempered by chastening experience. As a result of that, he was told, "You don't get to watch the test." Dad basically said, "Fine, screw you." He and Weinstock went back to Argonne and, consequently, my dad and Weinstock may well have gotten to live a few years longer by not being at the test, since it is my understanding that some people's lives were shortened by exposure. My dad was also thrilled that he was instead able to attend his first European conference.

Dad held sole patent on the tritium process he created, and because of that, they were able to produce fissionable hydrogen that led to the test at Bikini Atoll in 1950.

I didn't realize he played such a key role.

I gave Dad a present about fifteen years ago, some years before his open-heart surgery that put him in a coma for months. On eBay I'd found a black velvet pillow with gold fringe, with a map of Eniwetok and some fish, with a mushroom cloud representing a hydrogen-bomb explosion embroidered above the map of the island. He didn't like it because he considered black velvet pillowcases vulgar. After he died, I repossessed it. I'm actually very proud of his role in the H-bomb, because the hydrogen bomb is the most successful weapon ever produced that has never been used in anger. It kept the peace; it was frightening enough that it stopped the United States and the Soviet Union from going to war.

They could have used all the atom bombs that they have to keep from going to war.

They could have but they didn't. If there had been a war with atomic bombs it would have escalated to the hydrogen bomb, and the superpowers knew that. The fact that the hydrogen bomb was more horrific than the atom bomb kept the Cold War in balance, which kept the weapons used in peripheral conflicts to low-level conventional weaponry— even though we came close to using nukes a couple of times.

Of course the Soviet Union did too; we must not forget the Cuban missile crisis.

The United States considered dropping an A-bomb on Vietnam.

Yes, I know. That was after the Soviets were trying to place nuclear weapons in Cuba, ninety miles from our shore. There was posturing, but it never happened; and part of the reason was because the hydrogen bomb was hanging in the offing.

I never thought of it that way.

It's true that the horror and terror of having to escalate to the hydrogen bomb—the whole doomsday machine that they talked about in the movie Dr. Strangelove—actually did prevent a hot war between the United States and the Soviet Union. I am very proud of that; I figure that [Dad] was instrumental in keeping the peace for fifty years.

As far as the Lab was concerned, there were four ways which connected me to it that had nothing to do with the bomb itself. One was Dad's habit of blowing glass animals. He used to give Bubbe [our grandmother] checks rolled up inside little bodied animals. He'd make a little deer with a hollowed body out of a piece of Pyrex lab glass, and that would be the wrapping for a check.

I was becoming interested in rocks, and he brought me home a pestle from the Lab that was cracked so they couldn't use it. It might hold a trace element in the crack or something, but it was made out of gray agate. I still have it somewhere.

There was a chemical he brought home that was vermilion colored, which if you lit it would create its own volcano. In other words, it would spark and throw up a cone of ash like a volcano. This was when we were doing science projects in elementary school.

My brother was being troubled by a bully in elementary school, and Dad decided to bring back some substance from the lab which smelled like all the dog shit in the world. This was intended as chemical warfare, the plan being that my brother would put some drops on the bully's seat; so he'd start to stink; but Dad spilled some of it when bottling it up and it stunk up his lab up so badly that he decided this was too powerful to put in the hands of a child.

So he didn't think of this before he decided to bottle it up and bring it home?

No, it was a way to try and use science to avoid a physical confrontation.

Not with children. Now that's really crazy.

I don't see it that way; I thought that in the abstract it was a good way to avoid fisticuffs.

Do you believe, from our experiences growing up and our fathers' involvement in the Project and their science careers, that you have a different outlook from other people?

Absolutely I have a different outlook; absolutely I see the world in different ways; and I wouldn't trade it for anything. It would have been good if I had learned to temper some of my emotions a little younger. [Laughter] But I consider myself extraordinarily fortunate because I consider, for one thing, that your father and mine were two of the smartest people I've ever known. I don't know about your dad but it seemed—through the good and the bad—it was great to see, because when I was younger there appeared to be nothing my dad couldn't do.

I think that is common with any child and his or her parent.

Yes, but on a higher level, except maybe when it came to playing the guitar and singing on key.

I completely agree with that. I will never forget your dad's boisterous off-key singing at Passover seders.

He could do neither of those things, and it bothered him—if, for no other reason, than that Feynman could actually play an instrument.

My dad played the clarinet very well; but the violin, not so well. The dog would howl and we would leave the house for an hour.

And he had some artistic skills!

Quite a bit. His brother Nate was an artist and my father took painting and drawing classes. He also had incredible athletic abilities. Of course it was impossible for him to live up to his own standards because nothing was ever good enough if it was not perfect.

I'm assuming that if there were problems with electricity in the house, he knew how to deal with them without even thinking about it. Even if he hired someone to do it, he knew what had to be done and why. In other words, these things were not mysteries.

Were you at the dedication for my dad's stone?

Yes, of course.

Toward the end of my dad's life I asked him, "As a scientist, what do you think about religion?" This was one of the last serious conversations we had. Dad said, "When I was young we used to believe that reason would vanquish irrationality," he said, "and we were wrong." Now for him to say he was wrong about anything was a huge admission.

I am sitting down; I am amazed he admitted that!

In other words, you can use the mind for some things, but if science tries to vanquish irrationality, all you get is bad science.

My father would get very exasperated with me and say, "How many times do I have to tell you, if you can't prove it, it can't be real." I remember having a conversation about science and religion on Yom Kippur one year and asked him how he could believe in God and science at the same time. I don't remember what he said; maybe he didn't really have a clear answer for himself. When you think about what they were doing to discover the atom, an unseen particle— and how you can prove that it exists—that was really to my mind, merging the two, science and religion or spirituality. They had faith that something existed that you couldn't see. They took that faith and turn it into hard science.

But all of that was not provable to them. Human rationality is like a universal solvent; the problem with a universal solvent is that it can dissolve anything that it touches. Religion is the only thing that has proved itself capable of containing the universal solvent of human irrationality sufficiently, so that this destructive force can occasionally be channeled for good. My dad said that it doesn't have a perfect record, but it has a better record than anything else. This meant, as far as I was concerned, that, although he was a rationalist in almost everything, he recognized towards the end of his life that rational thought had limits. He had to pay respects to the irrational and treat it properly in order to be able to control it and contain it. I think it's a profound observation.

Belief in things that don't fall into the realm of religion can be just as powerful, important, and proven.

Religion has not been proved, because it's irrational; it's an irrational solution for an irrational impulse. He was saying that religion could contain the irrationality—an irrational concept containing irrationality, so it's a double negative.

[I wonder if the double negatives create a positive with regards to religion? Maybe this has something to do with Heisenberg's Uncertainty Principle.]

There is nothing wrong with that. Man has irrational impulses; and if religion can harness the irrational impulses to force people to, say, be charitable and take care of the sick and the poor, then it is taking those impulses, channeling them to godly belief, and thereby channeling them into a socially useful thing.

I agree with that, and if it is left at that, I think it is wonderful. But usually religion is not left at that.

Our dads had to prove it by mathematical and varying means.

Right, but by their own definition they didn't know that the atom existed, because you can't see it, touch it, or taste it.

That doesn't mean they didn't know it existed.

In their scientific view though, until they proved the atom, they didn't know it existed; they had to start with the concept, with Bohr.

Well, remember that, within your father's memory and mine, they disproved the concept of ether. Everything swimming through the ether, this ether was this invisible substance that existed in space. I'm not talking about ether the anesthetic.

I know.

The concept was that ether was connected to the music of the spheres—it was not mathematically proved that ether did not exist until sometime in the 1920s, well within their living memory, maybe later...

But my knowledge of the goals of science tells me they are looking for the proof of faith; that there are things that hold the universe together, that there are mathematical equations that will prove it.

Belief in God—just as when you get crazy enough on the left, you become far right.

I agree.

You can also end up getting into religion in weird ways if you get deeply enough into science.

A lot of ideas that were connecting concepts, like the Tao of physics [from The Tao of Physics *by Fritjof Capra]— I wouldn't say that that was crazy. If you get into anything too far, you have the opportunity to go crazy.*

Absolutely. What I take away from having grown up with all these ideas—and this is partly due to the unending skepticism of my father and yours, the fine contempt that they had for the more superstitious world that was not hooked into all of the scientific ideas—I look at things with a very hopefully clear, but certainly highly skeptical, view.

About ten years ago I was teaching a calligraphy class at my synagogue. It was in the autumn; Hiroshima Day happened to coincide with the class, and thus came up in the course of discussion. Someone started talking about how terrible it was that we dropped the bomb on Hiroshima. I contradicted her

vehemently. One of the things she said was that it was racist because we dropped it on Japan and not on Germany. I
said, "You have to understand something: Germany surrendered in April, and the bomb wasn't successfully tested until
August. A few days later is when they made the actual drops.
You don't usually drop weapons onto an enemy after they
have surrendered." Some of the scientists were talking about
a demonstration.

Actually Teller was in favor of that; he wanted a
demonstration.

He was wrong in that regard.

It was his opinion.

As far as the demonstration is concerned, Teller was
absolutely wrong. First of all, there was the process of exe-
cuting a demonstration. There was at least one reason it was
not practical. When you are in the midst of vicious hostilities
with an aggressive genocidal enemy, the chances that their
high command will come and take a peek at your demonstration with you is minimal.

Teller's idea was that once they saw how destructive it
was they would surrender, because they were on the verge of
surrendering anyway.

Understand this: how are you going to get them to look
at the demonstration when they are not going to be guests of
the belligerent?

They were going to do it 20,000 feet over Japan. Well,
maybe you're right.

If you are in the midst of hostilities and you prove to
someone that you have a weapon of unparalleled destruction and you don't use it, all you prove is that you don't have

the will to use it. What that does, instead of dampening their ardor, is to increase it; because it says you have a failure of will.

There is another aspect to it. They didn't know for sure that the bombs would work. They did the test at Trinity. That was a stationary test closely monitored with the scientists and the equipment there to test it. That's very different from transporting a bomb, putting it in an airplane, dropping it out of an airplane, and knowing it is going to go off. There are many traditional conventional bombs that people still find in Europe and other places that were duds. There were many nuclear weapons that were found that did not detonate that fell out of planes on the east coast of the United States and off the coast of Spain. They didn't know that a bomb dropped would hit and explode. If you do a demonstration and [it] doesn't come off, it looks bad. The other thing was that we only had two bombs, though fortunately, the Japanese didn't know that. We had the plutonium bomb and the uranium bomb. I forget which one was which at this point.

The uranium bomb was the one that was dropped over Hiroshima and the plutonium bomb was used on Nagasaki.

Much of my dad's career was based on discovering the properties of helium-3. He told me that he had to falsify certain data when he published papers in scientific journals because he discussed certain amounts of helium-3. The Soviets, by reading those papers, could figure out the number of hydrogen bombs from the quantity of helium-3 that was mentioned. So there was a security aspect even in that.

His career centered on exploring these properties and seeing how close he could get to absolute zero. That was all an outgrowth of the tritium process, which was produced in

1950. Even though Teller gave him the personal go-ahead to develop the tritium process, he still felt that Teller was the evilest man he ever met.

I've heard before that is how many people felt about him. Did he give a reason? I know my father hated him.

Never gave a reason; never said why. He liked Szilard. He thought Fermi was God basically. He liked everyone else in that generation. He wanted to be Feynman. But he did not like Teller.

Teller was giving a talk in Palm Springs when I was visiting my mother there during one of her escapes from the cold Chicago winters after my father died. I asked her if she wanted to go. She looked at me like she couldn't believe I would even consider the possibility. She said something about how horrible he was.

Have you read Paul Fussel's excellent essay, "Thank God for the Atom Bomb?"

No. [I did read it later.]

You should. It wasn't until after the Nagasaki bomb that the Japanese surrendered. They didn't surrender after Hiroshima, and there was, I believe, a week between the two bombs. Ten thousand people died in ordinary conventional warfare—in ordinary shelling, bombing, torpedoing, etcetera—in that period of time in which the Japanese did not surrender. They didn't stop until they got hit a second time and finally decided they had better stop before we dropped a third one.

I'm sure you know what the casualties would have been, mainly on the Allied side, if they had gone ahead with the Japanese ground invasion. Fussel writes about this in his essay. He was with the 45th Division in Europe and was wounded to be considered 45% disabled after the war, and got the appropriate compensation as a result. Despite being that disabled, he was being trained as part of the force that was going to go in during the home-island ground invasion. They were being told, we do not expect anyone in the five waves to make it ashore alive. You have some idea of what that means in human cost—you think about that—and then he wrote about what it must have been like for some of these people who had already survived some of the other island warfare—Peleliu, Tarawa, and Okinawa. They knew they were being groomed for the Japanese home-island invasion, knowing that there was an overwhelming chance that they were going to be cut down on the beaches. When they heard the second bomb hit and the Japanese surrendered, there was an overwhelming sense of relief.

Fussel also mentions that, if there had been a home-island invasion, the Japanese presiding over prison camps in Malaysia and other places had orders to massacre all of their prisoners. The shock and surrender that resulted from the two bombs was so overwhelming that all of those prisoners were saved as well, because the order to kill them was not given. That's not to mention the fate of all the Japanese civilians who were being groomed for home-island defense.

People talk about the terrible cost of Hiroshima and Nagasaki, but let's not forget that they are thriving cities today. Hundreds of thousands, if not a million, on each side were saved because of the people who were killed by the atomic blast, and I have no problem with that. Yes, it's horrific and tragic, but war is horrific and tragic. Truman made a statement about using the bomb to shorten the agony of young Americans.

I'm proud of what they did. They were twenty-two-year-olds unlocking the secrets of the universe, so of course they were thrilled to a part of such an important project.

Sometimes [I feel] that I'm the only sighted person walking around in a bunch of blind people.

I feel that way a lot.

This manifests itself many ways. No matter how much either of us did not learn any of the scientific principles that our fathers understood, there is still an attitude towards the world that we were brought up with. We grew up with a totally different view of the world than most other people. The concept was that when you confront something, you don't shrug your shoulders and just leave it to the experts. Whatever the problem is, examine it, analyze it, think your way through it, and solve it. There is a deep level of analysis, as an attitude, that goes on with the concepts we were brought up with, even if you or I did not learn certain specific scientific concepts themselves.

Because that was their thought process, they expected us to not only be exposed to it but think that way as well. It was taken as a given that you read great literature and had at least nodding acquaintance with great music—the idea that we are unlockers of the secrets of the universe, and therefore nothing is strange to us. We look at all physical things and look to see what is their skeleton, what's their root, what's behind them. We were brought up to have this as a habit and, as a result, we are incredibly blessed among humans—and cursed. It is both the curse of Cassandra—to speak the truth and not be believed—but also a blessing, because it means that you are blessed with sight and the ability to see things in and around you and respond to them, if you choose to, in a way that is totally different from the normal ruck of humanity. You know.

I know and maybe I wish I didn't, which of course is the point.

I told my father once that he was extraordinarily favored among men because he was able to go into science at the one time in human history when there was money for independent research.

My father said that also, and he tried to discourage my brother when he went to UC Berkeley for theoretical physics, because there was no future in it; there was no money. And David did leave the program and went to medical school.

When Dad was doing some teaching in 1989 at the Technion in Haifa, we went as a family on a trip to Israel. We saw ruins and beautiful mosaic floors, and other fascinating places. Dad was measuring the beading on some of the fallen lintels. There were small carved patterns and, from a distance, they all looked regular—but of course were not, because they were hand-carved by stonecutters thousands of years ago. He measured them because it fascinated him. He was amazed at both how similar they were and how much they varied. We got into a discussion about how they were meant to be viewed from a distance of ten-to-fifteen feet and the eye corrects for that at a distance so that, despite their being somewhat irregular, they still look even—and the present but unseen irregularity made them more pleasing than if they were truly regular, because there was this slight variation.

They were replicating nature by including a slight

variation.

Yes-though probably not intentionally. He went on about how an oak leaf "knows how" to grow like an oak leaf. I said, "Well, DNA." He said, "That's not enough of an answer, because how does it know to grow a certain number of points and grow this far before it curves in and curves out and then curves in again?" He said, "This is mind-boggling." He'd pass by an oak leaf, and everything like that was a source of wonder and curiosity. He was able to pass that on—maybe not his knowledge, maybe not his ability to analyze everything like that; but being able to look at something and, whether it's manmade or part of the natural world, and ask how does it tap into something else? How does it relate to something else; what does it do; what does it mean; where does it connect; what else is it connected to? He was constantly thinking about ideas like that. I think about things like that all the time-but not even consciously, half the time. I come out with stuff and people say, where did you come up with that? And you may say, "Doesn't everybody do that?" Everybody doesn't!

That's true; sometimes I read my poetry and people say, where did you come up with that? I never thought of that. Or, I put ideas and concepts together and people look at me like I am from another planet.

Searching for the connections, for the fundamental principle of their existence—to the extent that everyone in our family inherited that, simply because we grew up with that, and it was part of the natural embryonic fluid in which we were raised—makes us different from other people. Aside from the politics—and, as I said, I was proud of what they did during the war and what they did afterward—the attitude they conveyed about how to approach life is absolutely something that I cannot imagine living without. I can't imagine how immensely poorer my life would have been if I had not been brought up with that. It means you can be living, God forbid, in a blank cell somewhere and you still have resources. Better that you shouldn't be, but if you have a mind which is capable of thinking about word games, interconnections, numbers, seeing patterns, about all of these kinds of things, it means you are never, ever without resources. How great a gift is that?

True, but I wish it had been with less yelling.

Yeah what, you want jam on both sides?

Yes!

Well, the thing is, we didn't get it that way.

No kidding.

Chapter 25

Conclusion

"The end is where we start from."
—*T.S. Eliot*

The end of this book finds us back at the beginning, contemplating the stories of these "children of the bomb" and what they have to say to those of their own and future generations. Although this was a small cohort group with no controls, certain commonalities emerged. These stories tell of pride in our parents' accomplishments, secrets kept from us, confusion, anger, sadness, shame, and death—during and after the Project.

Many of those I interviewed were in Los Alamos, New Mexico; Oak Ridge, Tennessee; or Berkeley, California, as children during the war. Wendy lived at China Lake Naval Air Weapons Station after the war. In addition to being affected by the creation and use of the bomb and the Holocaust during the Second World War, we were, to a greater or lesser extent, traumatized by the war in Vietnam. I was more affected by this legacy of tragedy than were my siblings or cousins.

Perfection was a necessity for those who worked on the Project but had its cost, both for the scientists and for their children. For example, Glenn's most difficult challenge in life was measuring his achievements by how much his father accomplished in record time as a teenager on the Project. In my extended family doing your best was not enough. Reactions varied from my virtually giving up at a young age, to my older sister and brother earning straight A's and being valedictorian and top debater, my cousins studying at top schools, and later becoming high-achieving lawyers and an economist. My brother became a physician after pursuing theoretical physics in the same graduate school where Oppenheimer and Teller had taught.

This book was a journey into a moment in history that still defines our world. All the people I talked with had strong opinions about the further development of nuclear weaponry, believing that the A-bomb, (let alone the H-bomb or neutron bomb) should never again be used. All shared a sense of pride in the importance and legacy of science. All were exposed to and encouraged to participate in music, art, literature, and intellectual conversation and pursuits as children and were committed to making the world a better place through the arts, literature, religion, psychology, the law, physics, biology, chemistry, medicine, or environmental science. Some combined their interests in several fields: my sister has been a writer/editor and a birth-and-death doula; Daniel is an artist/cartoonist and a lawyer; Barbara combined art and science in the field of environmental design; Wendy worked as an art therapist; and I am a poet and photographer and have worked in sleep medicine and counseling.

The legacy of psychological and physical effects lingered, for myself and others. Most strikingly, how do you erase the emotional impact of seeing a scene of Armageddon as a child of twelve and a murder/suicide of your parents as an adult? Dana could not.

Some of the parents had a seeming casualness towards their work and children. Barbara's dad allowed her to take trinitite to school. My uncle contemplated bringing a vial of chemicals for his son to put on the chair of a boy who was bothering him. Only after some spilled when he was bottling it did my uncle decide it was too powerful to put in the hands of a child. The most striking example, however, was Dana's dad taking him to Trinity just weeks after the A-test, when the site was extremely radioactive.

As Kristi's father bravely and with dedication to his work and country ran out to shut off the valves at the secret lab on a Berkeley hill, he must have known he was sacrificing his health. In that moment he not only saved the city and surrounding area from a radiation leak but changed his daughter's future.

Some images and memories particularly stand out for me: Carol's wish for a bomb shelter for Christmas; twelve-year-old Dana standing on his toes, trying to peak over the top of a crater-a surreal place of green trinitite glass tinged with red from the tower and a punched-in barren ground that lay in the desert. The hovering ghost of a mushroom cloud led us all straight into the Cold War.

The scene from the opera *Doctor Atomic*, with the infant being rocked under the bomb tower brought forth in me a similar dread as finding the photos of the A-test at Bikini Atoll in my father's closet and seeing the photo of the pennant from the Canadian nuclear-power plant over my crib. They all had a chilling resonance deep within my consciousness.

As I envision the landscape the "children" experienced, I picture the towns and laboratories that were not on any map, fenced military enclosures stretching across the country from

New York to Tennessee, Illinois, New Mexico, and Washington. I see thousands of scientists working through the night, tens of thousands of workers performing jobs that were, to them, of an unknown purpose, but proud they were helping the war effort. I picture the workers, many of them women, as well as the scientists' and engineers' wives, finding out what they and their husbands had been working on with the rest of the world.

In my mind's eye I see the effects of the A-bombs—two cities destroyed, and the photos of the shadows on walls where a man stood, a child jumped, and leaves lay on the ground, all just moments before. I have seen the geometric shapes of a plateau in a desert, a round apartment building, cyclotrons, linear accelerators, and Ground Zero.

I see Dana and me standing as adults in a desolate place in New Mexico—where we had journeyed from two coasts—near the basin of Jornada del Muerta (Journey of Death) on the edge of white sands with no ocean in sight. This empty crater in the desert on a military installation is a gravesite—its headstone, an obelisk marking the birth of the Atomic Age. I remember the silent plea I uttered in front of the stone pyramidal structure:

"We are struggling for the survival and peace of the human race and our world. If we can again bring together the brilliance, talent, commitment, resources, and unlimited funds of the Manhattan Project in a Project Planet Earth—not to end a war, but to mark the beginning of an age of peace, maybe the human race and planet would have a chance to survive and thrive."

I placed a stone at the bottom of the pyramid, as you would at a Jewish gravesite as a remembrance. When we went to visit my mother's grave, my aunt (Daniel, Jesse, and Abigail's mother) said it is like leaving a calling card—a rock that is eternal.

Dana carried a jar of trinitite with him from the first atomic bomb blast at Trinity to the 60th anniversary reunion, Barbara brought some to school for show and tell, and my brother had pieces given to him by our father. Symbolically, I believe, we all will carry a piece of trinitite with us into the future if and until all 15,913 nuclear weapons that currently reside in nations throughout the world are decommissioned and banned.

I carry in my Danish knapsack the stories and connections of those who I reached out to and who reached back. Although my favorite memory of Copenhagen was of the Little Mermaid in the North Sea harbor and one of my favorite memories with my dad was watching Danny Kaye play Hans Christian Andersen in the movie of the same name, if I could, I would say to Issac Rabi, "Yes, I would have liked to have mermaids instead of the atomic bomb."

But, this is neither a fairy tale, a movie, nor science fiction. It is a tale of our world and the shadow that still lurks in underground storage facilities, clouding our hearts and minds. It is the story of my life and of other lives lived in the shadow of the bomb. A friend said to me, "Your book must have been a labor of love."

Yes, a labor of love while dreaming of peace.

> *"The words fill my head*
> *And fall to the floor*
> *If God's on our side*
> *He'll stop the next war."* [52]
> —Bob Dylan

Epilogue

Poems by the Author

Infinite

Deep in the desert sand
A hidden bunker is silent.

On a cold cement floor
A small girl curls up next to a
Stagnant atomic creation.

Never alive,
Never dead,
Wrapped in a repeating decade of a
Hallowed dream of limbo.

The casing reflects nothing
Of its inner core-
Waiting to be either disassembled or released
From its underground home.

The girl wakes,
Walks unsteadily toward a bomb
That points upward
To a galaxy of infinite possibilities.

She circles,
Like an Orthodox Jewish woman
Slowly walking around the groom
Seven times, in front of the chuppah.

She wonders if there is a world
Where the dead do not walk next to her,
Realizes the irony
Is grateful for the only song she has ever known.

Then dances
In the crater
Where the universe was discovered,
In invisible tracings
Of a scattered promise.

Haiku

A broken atom
Hotter than a thousand suns
Into the cold war

Interview-Inspired Poems

Water and Silk Don't Mix
Kristi Grove (Chapter 14)

Water and silk don't mix,
Like spying and trust
And silk dresses
No one could afford.

Water and silk don't mix,
Like the military
And scientists
Searching
For the secrets to the universe.

Water and silk don't mix,
Like straws of unequal length
That marked a man's fate

When a lottery chose whose life
Hung in the balance
And a daughter drew the line.

Perfection
Glen Klein (Chapter 19)

There was the light,
The heat,
And the pulse.

Then the youngest person at the test
A teenager could see
Through his hands.

Not a magic show
By his sixteen-year-old friends
In a garage.

It was perfection partly created,
And witnessed,
By the only person still alive

Who was that close
To the light, the heat, and the pulse.

Perfection,
A secret legacy.
On a grand scale.

Set forever in the mind of his son.

Echoes of a perfect light,
And the heat,
And pulse.

*"**Let the words be yours, I am done with mine.**"*

Words by John Barlow [53]

Endnotes

[1] **Cassidy.** Words by John Barlow. Music by Bob Weir. Copyright © 1972 ICE NINE PUBLISHING CO., INC. Copyright Renewed. All Rights Administered by Universal Music Corp. All Rights Renewed. *Used by Permission. Reprinted by permission of Hal Leonard Corporation.*

[2] **Box of Rain.** Words by Robert Hunter. Music by Phil Lesh. Copyright © 1970 ICE NINE PUBLISHING CO., INC. Copyright Renewed. All Rights Administered by Universal Music Corp. All Rights Renewed. Used by Permission. *Reprinted by permission of Hal Leonard Corporation.*

Chapter 2
[3] Itamar Yaoz-Kest, Israeli author (1934-).

[4] Stern, A. (2012, July 3). Best evidence yet found for "God particle": U.S. physicists. *Reuters.* Retrieved from http://www.reuters.com/article/us-usa-higgs-idUSBRE8610RK20120703.

Chapter 5
[5] Frayn, Michael. *Copenhagen.* New York: Anchor Books, 1998. Print.

[6] Ibid.

[7] "The principle of quantum mechanics, formulated by Heisenberg, that the accurate measurement of one of two related, observable quantities, as position and momentum or energy and time, produces uncertainties in the measurement of the other." Retrieved from http://www.dictionary.com.

[8] Frayn, Michael. *Copenhagen.* New York: Anchor Books, 1998. Print, 3.

Chapter 6
[9] Lao-tzu (604 – 531 b.c.e.), Chinese philosopher and founder of Taoism.

[10] *Desolation Row* by Bob Dylan Copyright © 1963 by Warner Bros. Inc.; renewed 1991 by Special Rider Music.

[11] *With God on Our Side* by Bob Dylan Copyright © 1963 by Warner Bros. Inc.; renewed 1991 by Special Rider Music.

Chapter 7

[12] Nuclear Energy at the University of Chicago. Retrieved from http://www.atomicarchive.com/Photos/Journey/HM_image1.shtml

[13] Steinberg, E. (1985), Radiochemistry of the Fission Products, *Journal of Chemical Education*, 66(5), 367-372.

Chapter 8

[14] A cyclotron is a circular particle accelerator in which charged subatomic particles generated at a central source are accelerated, spiraling outward to a fixed magnetic field by an alternating electric field. It is capable of generating particle energies between a few million and several tens of millions of electron volts.

[15] Retrieved from http://www.ne.anl.gov/pdfs/white_deer_fact_sheet.pdf

Chapter 9

[16] Live Science Staff. (July 15, 2015). Facts about plutonium. *Live Science*. Retrieved from www.livescience.com/39871-facts-about-plutonium.html.

[17] Koppes, S. (2016). How the first chain reaction changed science. *University of Chicago Newsletter*. Retrieved from http://www.uchicago.edu/features/how_the_first_chain_reaction_changed_science/.

[18] Retrieved from http://www.armscontrol.org.

Chapter 10

[19] Element 92, uranium, was named after the planet Uranus. The first two manmade elements—93, neptunium, and 94, plutonium—were named after the next planets in our solar system. Although Pluto has been reclassified as a dwarf planet, its namesake, plutonium, would

change our world forever.

[20] The Los Alamos Historical Archives has no official record of this process.

[21] *Survival under Atomic Attack: The Official U.S. Government Booklet*, 1950.

[22] Ibid.

[23] *Chance for Peace* speech was an address by U.S. President Dwight D. Eisenhower on April 16, 1953, shortly after the death of Soviet dictator Joseph Stalin.

Chapter 12
[24] See article in the index titled Battle over *Livermore Lab name widow says founder wouldn't approve of laboratory's role from the San Jose Mercury News*–September 30, 1987.

[25] *Physics in the Contemporary World*, Arthur D. Little Memorial Lecture at M.I.T. (25 November 1947).

Chapter 13
[26] Wallin, W. (2015) *Pomegranate Jelly*. Bloomington, IN: Xlibris.

[27] Ray tracing is a method for calculating the path of waves or particles. In physics it is used for analyzing optical systems.

Chapter 15
[28] There was no description of what kind of work Carol Caruthers's father did for the Manhattan Project, only his name, Stanley Blazyk, listed on the Manhattan Project Heritage website.

[29] The first Soviet nuclear test took place on August 29, 1949. United States was shocked that the Soviets had created and tested the bomb so soon. Even though they did not test another bomb for two-and-a-half years, this was essentially the start of the Cold War. Carol's father must have been trying not to scare her since he had to know the process had already begun.

Chapter 16

[30] Kistiakowsky was in charge of creating explosive lenses during the development of the plutonium bomb. He was a professor of physical chemistry at Harvard and later President's Eisenhower's Science Advisor.

[31] The certificates of anyone born or married at the Los Alamos site during the war years identified the place only as P.O. Box 1663.

[32] Fermi, L. (1954) *Atoms in the Family: My Life with Enrico Fermi.* Chicago, IL: The University of Chicago Press.

[33] Sundt Apartments were built during the Manhattan Project at Los Alamos. Many of the scientists and their families lived in them.

Chapter 17

[34] In 1894 at the summit of Ben Nevis (the highest mountain in Great Britain at 4,409 feet), Scottish physicist Charles Thomson Rees Wilson began developing expansion chambers for studying cloud formation. In 1912 he invented the cloud chamber, a sealed environment containing supersaturated vapor of water or alcohol. His chamber made ionizing radiation tracks visible for the first time.

[35] The Nuclear Threat Initiative was founded in 2001 and works "to prevent catastrophic attacks with weapons of mass destruction and disruption nuclear, biological, radiological, chemical, and cyber." http://www.nti.org.

Chapter 18

[36] Seaborg, G. T., and Seaborg, E. (2001). *Adventures in the Atomic Age: From Watts to Washington.* New York, NY: Farrar, Straus, and Giroux.

[37] The theme song from the 1959 movie *On the Beach*, a based on the book of the same title by Nevil Shute © 1957 about the aftermath of nuclear war after the nuclear cloud descended on Australia, the last place where humans remained alive.

[38] From the White House tape recordings, April 25, 1972. Retrieved

from http://www.nytimes.com/2002/03/01/world/nixon-proposed-using-a-bomb-in-vietnam-war.html

[39] Seaborg was the principal or co-discoverer of ten elements: americium, curium, berkelium, californium, einsteinium, fermium, mendelevium, nobelium and element 106, which, while he was still living, was named seaborgium in his honor. He also discovered more than 100 atomic isotopes and he developed the extraction process used to isolate the plutonium fuel for the second atomic bomb. Retrieved from https://en.wikipedia.org/wiki/Glenn_T._Seaborg.

[40] In 1954 Seaborg became associate director of the Radiation Laboratory. (It eventually would become Lawrence Berkeley National Lab.) In 1958 he was appointed UC Berkeley's chancellor, a position he relinquished after three years when President Kennedy asked him to chair the Atomic Energy Commission (AEC). In 1971 he returned to Berkeley and resumed teaching, which he continued until 1979.

[41] The Stockpile Stewardship and Management Program is a U.S. Department of Energy program to test nuclear capabilities without actually performing a nuclear test. This program has been in place since 1996.

[42] *Learning to Glow: A Nuclear Reader*, ed. John Bradley, University of Arizona Press, ©2000.

[43] The Norwegian rocket incident, known as the Black Brant scare, took place on January 25, 1995, off the northwestern coast of Norway. The rocket carried scientific equipment to study the aurora borealis. It reached the height of 1,453 kilometers (903 miles), the height of a U.S. Navy submarine-launched Trident missile. Russia feared a high-altitude nuclear attack that could have blinded their radar. Russian nuclear forces were put on high alert, and president Boris Yeltsin had to decide whether to launch a nuclear barrage against the United States. (*"Norwegian Rocket Incident, Wikipedia: the Free Encyclopedia*. Retrieved from https://en.wikipedia.org/wiki/Norwegian_rocket_incident, accessed March 17, 2015.)

Chapter 19

[44] The first nuclear power plant that began creating electricity for commercial use was APS-1 on June 26, 1954 in Obninski, Russia at the Institute of Physics and Power Engineering.

[45] Lanouette, W. (2009, May). Civilian Control on Atomic Weaponry. *Arms Control Association*. Retrieved from https://www.armscontrol. org/act/2009_5/Lanouette.

[46] Jumbo was originally 214 tons, 28 feet long, and 12 ft. 8 in. in diameter, with a steel wall up to 16 in. thick. It was shaped like a thermos and designed to hold the plutonium core of Trinity if there was a misfire.

[47] In 1960, a B-52 collided with a tanker over Palomares, Spain, while refueling, and its four atomic bombs fell to earth. Three B28, formally Mark 28, bombs that fell on land were quickly recovered, but the fourth fell into the sea and was recovered only after a lengthy search. Two bombs were destroyed when their conventional explosives detonated; the surviving two bomb casings are on display at the museum in Albuquerque, New Mexico.

Chapter 21

[48] The Atoms for Peace conference took place in Geneva, Switzerland, on September 1-13, 1958. It was the second conference of its kind sponsored by the United Nations and was attended by 5,000 scientists and government officials from around the world. The secret research that had been done on fusion power was the topic of the conference and introduced as an energy promise for the future. The conference officially initiated an era of scientific communication and ended the classification of research and documents that had carried over from WWII.

Chapter 22

[49] Abraham, B.M. (1963), U.S. Patent No. 3100184, Washington, D.C. U.S. Patent and Trademark Office.

Chapter 24

[50] Phosgene is a chemical compound with the formula COCl. This colorless gas gained infamy as a chemical weapon during World War I during which it was responsible for about 85% of the 100,000 deaths caused by chemical weapons.

[51] "Tritium is a hydrogen isotope with two neutrons. Deuterium has one neutron. Although tiny amounts occur naturally from cosmic ray bombardment, tritium is produced in nuclear reactors by neutron capture by lithium and subsequent decay into helium and tritium." – Described by my brother, David Steinberg.

Chapter 25

[52] *With God on Our Side* by Bob Dylan Copyright © 1963 by Warner Bros. Inc.; renewed 1991 by Special Rider Music.

Epilogue

[53] **Cassidy**. Words by John Barlow. Music by Bob Weir. Copyright © 1972 ICE NINE PUBLISHING CO., INC. Copyright Renewed. All Rights Administered by Universal Music Corp. All Rights Renewed. Used by Permission. *Reprinted by permission of Hal Leonard Corporation.*

Appendix

First two pages of the patent awarded to my uncle, Bernard M. Abraham, for tritium production, a process critical in the development of the hydrogen bomb.

US3100184-Tritium production by neutron-irradiation of aluminum-lithium alloys

Publication number	US3100184 A
Publication type	Grant
Publication date	Aug 6, 1963
Filing date	Sep 24, 1951
Priority date	Sep 24, 1951
Publication number	US 3100184 A,
	US 3100184A,
	US-A-3100184,
	US3100184 A,
	US3100184A
Inventors	Bernard M Abraham
Original Assignee	Bernard M Abraham
Export Citation	BiBTeX,
	EndNote,
	RefMan
Non-Patent Citations (1), Referenced by (4), Classifications (9)	
External Links:	USPTO,
	USPTO Assignment,
	Espacenet

Tritium production by neutron-irradiation of aluminum-lithium alloys
US 3100184 A

Abstract available in

Images(3)

Claims available in

Description (OCR text may contain errors)

ing an aluminum-lithium alloy body,

United States Patent Office 3,100,184 TRITIUM PRODUCTION BY NEUTRON-IRRADEA- TION F ALUMINUM-LITHIUM ALLOYS Bernard M. Abraham, Chicago, 111., assiguor to the United States of America as represented by the United States Atomic Energy Commission No Drawing. Filed Sept. 24, 1951, Ser. No. 248,105 12 Claims. (Cl. 204154.2)

This invention deals with the production of tritium by neutron-irradiation of lithium, and in particular of the lithium isotope having a mass number of 6. Natural lithium contains 7.35% of the Li isotope. Tritium is the hydrogen isotope having a mass number of 3; it is radioactive and therefore valuable as a tracer in the study of reactions involving hydrogen.

San Jose Mercury News (CA)

Battle Over Livermore Lab Name Widow Says Founder Wouldn't Approve Of Laboratory's Role

September 30, 1987

Molly Lawrence's quest to dissociate her husband's name from the nuclear weapon laboratory he helped found in Livermore 35 years ago is nearing a showdown in the U.S. Congress.

An amendment erasing the "Lawrence" from Lawrence Livermore National Laboratory is included in a defense authorization bill passed by the House of Representatives but not in the companion bill under consideration in the Senate. As a result, the name change will be one of the items -- a minor one -- on the negotiating table in a week or so when a House-Senate conference committee works out a compromise version of the bills.

One of the committee members from the House will be Rep. Ronald Dellums, D-Oakland, who added the name change to the House bill. One of those on the other side of the table will be Sen. Pete Wilson, R-San Diego, who was asked by "some people at the lab" to keep the name the way it is, according to an aide. Ernest O. Lawrence was a Nobel Prize-winning physicist who worked on the atomic bomb during World War II and helped found the Livermore laboratory in 1952 in large part to further research on the hydrogen bomb. He died in 1958. His widow, who still lives in their Berkeley home, has become disillusioned with the laboratory's role in the arms race and says her husband, were he alive, would want his name removed from the lab's title.

She has tried for several years, beginning with the University of California Board of Regents, which manages the lab for its owner, the U.S. Department of Energy. Never before, however, has the issue advanced this far in Congress.

The director of the lab, Roger Batzel, opposes the name change. The issue was brought to Wilson's attention during a tour of the lab this summer, according to Otto Bos, his director of public affairs. "A number of people at the lab would prefer not to have the name of the lab changed," Bos said Tuesday.

"Having his name on the lab is prestigious."

"Sen. Wilson is keeping an open mind," Bos said, and implied that the name change could become a bargaining chip during negotiations. "There are a number of issues they (Wilson and Dellums) are going to have to discuss, such as the (USS) Missouri."

Dellums has opposed making San Francisco the home port of the recommissioned battleship Missouri; Wilson, a Missouri supporter, was on board as a guest during the recommissioning ceremonies.

The name change, if it passes, would not affect the name of Lawrence Berkeley Laboratory, also named after E.O. Lawrence

Deborah Leah Steinberg is the daughter and niece of scientists that worked at the University of Chicago Metallurgical (Met) Lab a branch of the Manhattan Project during WWII, the secret project that researched and developed the first atomic weapons.

Leah has degrees in Anthropology, and Counseling Psychology with a career in research and clinical Sleep Medicine and counseling. She is a published poet, a nature photographer, a music lover, and loves to dance.

She lives in the San Francisco east bay area.

The Deadheads are doing the dance of life and this I would say, is the answer to the atom bomb."
—*Joseph Campbell*